WRITE NOW™

a complete self-teaching program for better handwriting

Barbara Getty and Inga Dubay

Continuing Education Press   Portland State University

To our sons, Todd Getty, and Christopher, Gregory and Jonathan Dubay

Thanks to Lloyd J. Reynolds for his inspirational teaching and writings,
and to our students for their desire for a legible and graceful handwriting.

By the same authors:

The Italic Handwriting Series. Continuing Education Publications.
Portland State University. Portland, OR. 1986.

Italic Letters: *Calligraphy & Handwriting*. Simon and Schuster, Inc.
New York. 1984.

WRITE NOW

Copyright 1991 Barbara Getty and Inga Dubay

First Edition 1991
Continuing Education Press
Portland State University
1633 S.W. Park Avenue, P.O. Box 1394
Portland, OR 97207

Printed in the United State of America

10   9   8   7   6   5   4   3   2

The following acknowledgements are gratefully made for permission
to print copyrighted material:
Pages (16), 23, & (23) from *The First Writing Book* by John Howard Benson,
Yale University Press, 1954; Chancery cursive, anonymous scribe, from The
Houghton Library, Harvard University, Department of Printing and Graphic
Arts; Round Hand, John Bickham, *The Universal Penman*, from *Lettering:
Modes of Writing in Western Europe from Antiquity to the End of the Eight-
eenth Century* by Hermann Degering, Taplinger/Pentalic, 1978.

Cataloging data:
1. Handwriting
652.0   Z43.G48   LC 90-80696
ISBN 0-87678-089-3

In the cities of the world, millions of typewriters, copy machines, fax machines, and word processors are cranking out endless streams of reams of paper in our effort to communicate the written word—to get information from one place to another.

Most of the words we read today are made by machine. But even in this computer age, the simple handwritten note is an essential part of everyday life. Children are required to use handwriting daily at school, and most adults use it daily in their work and in their personal lives — there will always be a need for handwriting.

Professional writing, from novels to newspaper articles, usually is done on word processors, but from a practical point of view, handwriting will persist in everyday use for two simple reasons—it is convenient and it is personal. A young woman working alone in a northwest forest fire lookout station complained that the letters sent by her family were printed by computer and were too impersonal. What's more, her brother didn't even bother to tear off the perforated edges or sign his name. She pleaded for handwritten messages. Handwriting counts!

Until the turn of the 20th century, handwriting was a major discipline in the classroom. In American schools, the general practice has been to introduce young students to a drawn manuscript alphabet known as "ball and stick."

Many of these letters require a cumbersome series of strokes.

manuscript: "ball and stick"

As students are just gaining some mastery of these forms, usually at the beginning of third grade they are asked to abandon their new skills and learn to write a different set of 52 letters known as "looped cursive." This frustrates and confuses many learners.

bridge *bridge*

manuscript   looped cursive

Paradoxically, the looped cursive that is generally taught in upper grades stems from letterforms inscribed by copperplate engravers and not from letters designed for handwriting. When these forms were taught as a major subject with hours of practice, an elegant hand could be the reward. But in this modern age, school systems are increasingly reluctant to devote much time to handwriting as a classroom course, and most teacher-training programs neglect instruction in handwriting. Consequently, handwriting is on the bottom rung of the educational ladder and in many instances deteriorates to the point of illegibility.

Many schools throughout the nation are now adopting italic, an old yet innovative, simple yet elegant approach to handwriting.

This contemporary italic hand-writing system presents one simple lower-case alphabet: <u>basic</u> <u>italic</u>. Note that these letters are cursive in nature from day one, since most of the letters are written in one stroke with no lift of the writing tool.

a b c d e f g h i
j k l m n o p q
r s t u v w x y z

BASIC ITALIC LOWER-CASE

<u>Cursive</u> <u>italic</u> retains the same letter forms and the writer merely joins them together—a sort of "joined printing." This eliminates the transition phase that tradition-ally occurs when changing from ball and stick to looped cursive.

a quick brown fox

BASIC ITALIC

a quick brown fox

CURSIVE ITALIC

Cursive italic capital letters retain their basic forms except for optional flourishes.

A B C D E F

BASIC CAPITALS

A B C D E F

CURSIVE CAPITALS

The lifetime ability to handwrite legibly is as important as the other basic aspects of communica-tion — reading, speaking and listening. But unfortunately, hand-writing is understressed and under-valued. An article in TIME magazine a few years ago stated that this country's estimated business losses due to illegible handwriting (hand-written instructions, bookkeeping figures, addresses, etc.) amount to $200 million a year.

Where interoffice memos & notes are written by hand, there is an awaken-ing to the need for a personal touch. Business executives are encouraged "to take a few minutes to write a handwritten note using the finest of fountain pens and stationery. The letter — not the fax, the phone, or the computer — is the heart and soul of networking."[1]

"It is interesting to note," says an-other writer, "that even with the invention of the typewriter, letters continue to be handsigned, and even memos are initialed. This aspect of writing will continue to play a role in our culture. It is difficult to imagine a time when love letters between young men and women will end up on floppy disks stored in an attic."[2]

For the last 5,000 years, cultures have been recording their history in written form; and although our system of communication known as handwriting may continue to undergo changes, it is here to stay — and those who want to leave a legible mark may find italic the way to write!

Barbara Getty and Inga Dubay

P O R T L A N D · O R E G O N

1. Don Wallace. "Sending the Right Message." SUCCESS Magazine, April, 1989, p. 62.
2. Keith Scoville. SIGN, SYMBOL, SCRIPT. University of Wisconsin, Madison, 1984, p.82.

CONTENTS

All letters written in one stroke unless otherwise indicated.

BASIC ITALIC

All letters start at the top and go down or over, except *d* and *e*.

Aa Bb Cc Dd Ee Ff Gg

Hh Ii Jj Kk Ll Mm

Nn Oo Pp Qq Rr Ss Tt

Uu Vv Ww Xx Yy Zz

0 1 2 3 4 5 6 7 8 9

or 4

All letters written in one stroke unless otherwise indicated.

CURSIVE ITALIC

Join all lower-case letters, except lift before *f* and *z* and lift after *g, j, q, e,* and *y.*

Aa Bb Cc Dd Ee Ff Gg

nan nbn ncn ndn nen nfn ngn

or nen

Hh Ii Jj Kk Ll Mm

nhn nin njn nkn nln nmn

Nn Oo Pp Qq Rr Ss Tt

nnn non npn nqn nrn nsn ntn

or nsn

Uu Vv Ww Xx Yy Zz

nun nvn nwn nxn nyn nzn

6

WRITE NOW is designed as a self-instructional course in basic and cursive italic handwriting with an introduction to italic calligraphy.

Italic is a modern handwriting system based on 16th century letterforms that first developed in Italy & later were also used in England and Europe. Since the early 1900's there has been a growing interest in italic in the United States, England, Sweden, and other countries.

Italic provides both the young person & the adult with letterforms that are highly suited to a rapid, legible handwriting. Italic is also an art form when written in formal calligraphy. "Calligraphy," from the Greek KALLI (beautiful) and GRAPHIA (writing) generally refers to letters carefully hand-written with a monoline or edged tool, often unjoined. Italic calligraphy is one type of formal hand lettering.

Certainly THE ART OF WRITING is the most miraculous of all things CARLYLE man has devised.

BASIC ITALIC HANDWRITING · pp. 13 - 26

Handwriting is a system of movements involving touch.

ALFRED FAIRBANK

CURSIVE ITALIC HANDWRITING · pp. 27-60

The history of writing is, in a way, the history of the human race...

FREDERICK W. GOUDY

CURSIVE ITALIC HANDWRITING · EDGED PEN · pp. 61-74

CALLIGRAPHY grasps the mind and makes the writing come alive

LLOYD J. REYNOLDS

ITALIC CALLIGRAPHY · EDGED PEN · p. 69

Writing is a system of conventional signs, and at any particular point in time, those using the system must be able to recognize the symbols and what they signify. The history of written symbols through the ages presents a fascinating story. The writing practice in this book incorporates a brief history of our writing heritage, and the introduction of cursive capitals includes the historical development of each letter.

HOW TO USE THIS BOOK

Read the introduction and obtain the writing tool of your choice: pen, pencil, or edged tool. Take a moment to study the information on each practice page before writing. Read a line of writing, trace the model letters, then write your own letters or words in the space provided below. <u>Do</u> write in this workbook!

By tracing the model letters on the page before writing them yourself, you may gain an awareness of finger and hand movements that will help you form the proper letter shapes.

BASIC ITALIC
waist line
a a a - d d d - e -
base line   imaginary branching line
a   d

CURSIVE ITALIC
trace:
an cn dn hn in
copy line above:

On pp. 89-96 you will find sample ruled pages which may be duplicated or may be used under a blank sheet of white paper for further practice.

When writing, be sure to begin all letters at the top, then go down or over to the left or to the right as the directional arrows indicate. Note that lower-case <u>d</u> begins at the waist line and the one-stroke <u>e</u> begins at the branching line. (If you are using a two-stroke <u>e</u>, it begins at the waist line.) Follow the directional arrows as shown on the model letters.

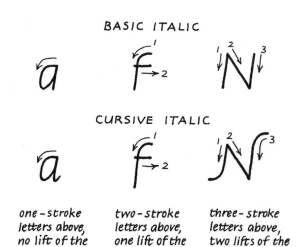

BASIC ITALIC

CURSIVE ITALIC

one-stroke letters above, no lift of the writing tool

two-stroke letters above, one lift of the writing tool

three-stroke letters above, two lifts of the writing tool

As you practice on your own, write a letter 3 or 4 times only — writing an entire line of one letter is of little value. Begin to write words and sentences as soon as possible.

WRITING TOOLS

MONOLINE TOOLS (*pp. 13–60*)
No. 2 pencil, medium or fine fiber tip pen, ballpoint, cartridge ink pen or fountain pen may be used to complete pp. 14–50. The line written with a monoline tool is of a constant thickness like this writing.

EDGED PENS (*pp. 61–74*)
Any edged fountain pen, fiber-tip pen, or dip nib approximately ¾ mm in width may be used to complete pp. 63–69. An edged tool may also be used for pp. 14–50. The line formed with the edged tool has thicks and thins.

These three lines are written with an edged pen.

Left-handed nibs are available for some cartridge ink pens, fountain pens, and dip nibs. The left-handed nib has a left-oblique edge.

(*See p. 62 for further information.*)

NOTE: *Cartridge and fountain pens hold their own ink supply. Dip nibs must be immersed in ink.*

HOW TO SIT

Rest your feet flat on the floor & keep your back comfortably straight for the best results. Rest your fore-arms on the writing surface. A flat surface is adequate for mono-line writing, but a slanted surface is more comfortable for both monoline & edged pen writing. Prop up one foot to avoid fatigue when writing for long periods of time.

flat surface

slanted surface

TOOL POSITION

Hold your monoline tool or edged pen with your thumb and index finger, resting it on your middle finger. Rest the shaft of the writing tool near the large knuckle.

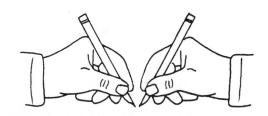

To relax hand, tap index finger on writing tool three times. Repeat as needed.

PAPER POSITION

If you are left-handed and write with the wrist below the line of writing, turn the book clockwise so it is slanted to the right as illustrated. If you are left-handed and write with a "hook" with the wrist above the line of writing, turn the book counter-clockwise so it is slanted to the left as illustrated. This is similar to the right-handed position.

(See p. 62 for edged pen paper position.)

If you are right-handed, turn the book counter-clockwise so it is slanted to the left as illustrated.

(See p. 62 for edged pen paper position.)

Hold your workbook or paper with your non-writing hand so that the writing area is centered in front of you. After you complete a line or two, move the writing surface up so that you are constantly writing in a comfortable position. Move your paper to suit your hand, not vice versa.

CHECKING YOUR WORK

The essential characteristics of legible handwriting include the following:

SHAPE – Do your letters look similar to the models in this book?

STROKE SEQUENCE – Are you writing the letters in the proper stroke sequence by following the directional arrows?

SIZE – Are you writing with a consistent body height? Are your ascenders and capitals 1½ times the body height of the letters?

SLOPE – Are you writing with a consistent letter slope?

SPACING – Are you writing letters close together within words? Are you leaving approximately the width of *n* between words?

SPEED – Is your speed consistent with your purpose?

FORMAL WRITING – essays, reports, thank you notes, business letters, applications, maps, signs, posters (the writing in this book).

INFORMAL WRITING – daily assignments, letters and notes to friends, rough drafts of poems, stories.

RAPID WRITING – grocery lists, note taking, phone messages, itemizing assignments.

(See GUIDELINES, pp. 52-55)

VOCABULARY

waist line | arch | Capital height | ascender height | exterior counter | cross-bar | downstroke | jot | horizontal join
base line | body or "x" height | branching line | entrance serif | exit serif | diagonal join
descender length | interior counter | 2-stroke letter-sans serif | 5° slope

BASIC ITALIC

A quick brown fox
jumps over the lazy dog.

CURSIVE ITALIC

A quick brown fox
jumps over the lazy dog.

EDGED-PEN ITALIC

A quick brown fox jumps over the lazy dog.

NOTES ON HANDWRITING

"Handwriting is for writing.... Parents and teachers nod approval for a crisp, well-crafted page, a good impression is made on a job application...all important elements, but they pale next to the substance they carry...agreements to free hostages...a love note, a diary, all take precedence over the script.

"Handwriting is the vehicle carrying information on its way to a destination. If it is illegible, the journey will not be completed. Handwriting, like skin, shows the outside of a person. But beneath the skin beats the living organism, the life's blood, the ideas, the information."[1]

1. Donald Graves. WRITING: TEACHERS & CHILDREN AT WORK. Heinemann Educational Books, 1983, p.171.

RELATED PUBLICATIONS
by the authors of WRITE NOW

ITALIC HANDWRITING SERIES: a comprehensive, self-directed hand-writing program for children & adults consisting of seven grade-level work-books (K-6), an instruction manual, blackline masters, classroom charts, desk strips & a moveable alphabet set.
Published by Continuing Education Press, Portland State University.

ITALIC LETTERS: Calligraphy & Handwriting: a "hands-on" manual that will enable you to develop a legible, graceful, and fluent edged pen calligraphic script. A history of writing is included.
Published by Prentice Hall Press, a division of Simon and Schuster.

Order the above books from Portland State University, Continuing Education Press. P.O. Box 1394, Portland. OR 97207. (503)725-4891. Toll free outside Oregon: 1-800-547-8887, ext. 4891.

PERSONAL HANDWRITING SAMPLES
Write your BEFORE and AFTER handwriting samples.

BEFORE

Before you begin this book, write the following sentence in your everyday handwriting. Also write your address and today's date.

A quick brown fox jumps over the lazy dog.

Write the sentence on lines 1 and 2.

1

2

Name

3

Address

4

5

Date

6

AFTER

After you have completed the basic and cursive sections of this book (to page 49), write the following sentence in cursive italic. Also write your address and today's date.

A quick brown fox jumps over the lazy dog.

Write the sentence on lines 1 and 2.

7

8

Name

9

Address

10

11

Date

12

PART ONE

Basic Italic
& Numerals

Lower-case
Capitals
Numerals
Writing Practice
Handwriting Tips

LOWER-CASE FAMILIES *according to similar shapes*

FAMILY *i j l · k or k v w x z · h m n r · u y · a d g q · b p · o e c s · f t*
1 2 3 4 5 6 7 8

These letters are presented at 9 mm body height to help you focus on the letter shapes, tool hold, and hand movements before moving to a smaller, more natural letter size.

Write all letters in one stroke without lifting your writing tool unless otherwise indicated. Trace each letter, then write your own in the space provided. Take note of letter families and shapes as you practice.

FAMILY 1 vertical strokes *(see vocabulary, p. 11)*

ascender height
waist line
branching line ... ↕ 9 mm body height
base line
descender height

FAMILY 2 diagonal strokes

cross x at branching line or slightly above

FAMILY 3 the arch

branching line

form arch by retracing downstroke back up to the branching line, then curve upward to the right

FAMILY 4 inverted arch

WRITING PRACTICE · *keep letters close together within words*

9mm

LOWER-CASE FAMILIES, continued

FAMILY 5 basic _a_ shape counter

begin horizontally

abrupt curve

a a d d g g q q

a d g q

FAMILY 6 inverted basic _a_ shape   **FAMILY 7** elliptical curves

b b p p   o o   e e

b p   o   e

begin _e_ at branching line   alternate 2-stroke _e_:

Family 7, continued   **FAMILY 8** _f_ and _t_ crossbar

c c s s   f f   t t

c s   f   t

WRITING PRACTICE · _a pangram_ (_a sentence containing all 26 letters of our alphabet_)

a quick brown fox

a

jumps over the lazy dog

j

9mm

Practice words and sentences on notebook paper, writing a space high. See pp. 68-69 for additional pangrams.

LOWER-CASE FAMILIES according to similar shapes (5mm body height)

i j l · k or k v w x z · h m n r · u y · a d g q · b p · o e c s · f t

FAMILY 1   2   3   4   5   6   7   8

All letters are written in one stroke with no pencil/pen lift unless otherwise indicated.

FAMILY 1
i j l

Trace & copy line above. (Fill each line on the page.)

i i i i i   j j j j   l l l l

i   j   l

RELAX

Exhale on downstroke. This may help you write straight lines.

FAMILY 2
k v w x z

k k   OPTION: or k k   v v   w w   x x   z z

k   k   v   w   x   z

Trace and write:

will will

FAMILY 3
h m n r

h h   m m   n n   r r

h   m   n   r

mix mix   rim rim

FAMILY 4
u y

u u   y y

u   y

FAMILY 5
a d g q

a a a   d d d

a   d

g g g   q q q

g   q

adding a

· PICTURE WRITING ·

As far as we know, about 20,000 B.C. people began painting pictures on the walls of the caves in which they lived. Paintings of bison, rhinoceroses, horses and bulls have been found in Spain and France. Early paintings and drawings show animals just standing, but later they are shown in action — the beginning of storytelling.

FAMILY 6
b p

b b   p p   bumpy

b   p   b

5mm

SELF-EVALUATION: Do your letters slope in the same direction?   bumpy

16

FAMILY 7
oecs

Trace & copy line above.

OPTION:

o o o   e e e   or   e e e

overlap stroke 2 over stroke 1

o   e   e

2-stroke e: See page 36, cursive Join 3, and page 57.

c c c   s s s

c   s

FAMILY 8
ft

f f f   t t t

t is a short letter!

f   t

· AMERICAN INDIAN SIGNS ·

bear tracks   mountains   rain clouds

tepee (tipi)   lightning

Before alphabets were developed, many peoples of the world used pictures to tell stories and to send messages and instructions.

ocean   tepee   clouds   mountains

ocean

ANGRAM a quick brown fox jumps over the lazy dog

G

SHAPE SLOPE SPACING STROKES

Trace & copy this paragraph.

Lower-case italic is based on the elliptical*

L

The diagonal lines at the right are sloped 5° to the right. Slope your writing from 0°- 15° to the right. Be consistent.

shape. The letters slope slightly to the

right and are closely spaced. Twenty one

Tracing letters gives you the feel of the letters and the correct spacing within words and between them.

of the letters are written in one stroke.

2-stroke letters

f f   i i   j j   t t   x x   OPTIONAL 2-STROKE e e   k k

5mm

*elliptical (i-'lip-ti-kəl): shaped like an ellipse — an oval having both ends alike: O

CAPITAL FAMILIES *according to similar letter widths*

CDGOQ · MW · AHKNTUVXYZ · EFILBPRSJ
WIDE   WIDEST   MEDIUM   NARROW

Trace and copy. Fill each line. (Capitals are 1½ times the body height of lower-case letters.)

WIDE

These letters are about as wide as they are tall.

WIDEST

Letters are wider than they are tall.

MEDIUM

Letters are about 4/5 as wide as they are tall.

· SUMERIAN PICTOGRAMS ·

ox   sun   house   (foot) stand go (Ideogram)

The most ancient system of writing we know of was used by the Sumerians who lived in Mesopotamia before 4,000 BC.

At first, like other cultures, they drew objects simply. Then, as shown above, the picture became a symbol of the object rather than the object itself. These symbols are called pictograms.

Symbols which represent ideas, like "day," "time," "go," "stand," are called ideograms.

Did you know we read and write capitals only about 2% of the time?

NARROW

NOTE: Stroke 3 lower than 3 on E   I is the narrowest capital

Letters are about half as wide as they are tall.

or   for rapid writing

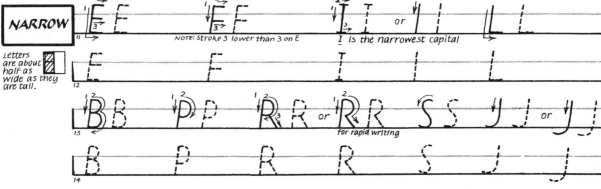

CAPITAL PRACTICE   MESOPOTAMIA · 4,OOO B.C.

height of caps

5mm

See Development of Our Alphabet on pages 76-83.

CAPITAL LETTERS (CAPS)

In addition to using caps with lower-case letters, plain caps may be used for headings, titles, posters, banners, addresses, abbreviations, certificates, etc.

LARGE CAPS

MEETING · 4 P.M. TODAY · ROOM 2

write P.M. shorter

notice of meeting

Cap height line

M

certificate title

HANDWRITING AWARD

Visualize the height of caps. They are 1½ times the body height.

H

SMALL CAPS

A B C D E F F G H I J or J K L M N

Small caps may be written wider than large caps.

A

O P Q R R S T U V W X Y E Z

FROM LATIN ET: AND

O

CAP PRACTICE

LARGE CAPS AND SMALL CAPS MAY BE USED SEPARATELY OR TOGETHER

Periods may or may not be used with many abbreviations.

RSVP · P.S. · A.M. P.M.

write a.m. and p.m. in lower-case unless using all caps

R

address

1345 NW CAPITAL

I

State and zip code should be written on the same line on envelopes.

PORTLAND OR 97286

P

MIXED CAPS

THE STORY OF HANDWRITING

by Alfred Fairbank · New York: Watson – Guptill, 1970

T

· CUNEIFORM WRITING ·

About 2500 B.C.

water   dwelling place (house)   mountain

About 1300 B.C.

B   G   P   stylus (writing tool)

(cuneiform - from Latin: cuneus - wedge, forma - shape)

The Sumerians generally wrote on damp clay tablets. Mistakes could be easily smoothed out, but it was difficult to draw curves or circles in the clay. So the scribes began using a wedge – shaped tool of wood, bone or metal which they pressed in the clay.

The use of cuneiform spread to other cultures, among them, Persians, Babylonians and Hittites.

The script finally appeared in one form as a genuine alphabet of 30 symbols in the ancient city of Ugarit in northern Syria.

5mm

SELF-EVALUATION: Are your large caps 1½ times the body height of lowercase letters? body height E 1½ times body ht.

NUMERALS
The word NUMBER stands for an idea—how many objects in a certain group.
The word NUMERAL describes the symbol we use for the number idea.

Just as the first writing happened long after people began speaking, writing numerals to represent
numbers came long after people began counting. The earliest numerals known were
marks on stones and notches in sticks.

About 3,400 B.C. the Egyptians developed a written number system using hieroglyphics, as shown:

coiled rope ~ 100   How would we write this? _____

One problem with the Egyptian system and those of the Greeks and the Romans is that none of them had
a symbol to represent zero, "not any." In most early systems, people formed numerals by
repeating a few basic symbols, then adding their values.

The numerals we use most likely came by way of Arabia from a starting point in India. The Hindus of
India had a superior system— it had a base of 10 and symbols for each number from one to
nine. This was about 300 B.C. Probably about 900 years later they invented a symbol for
zero. However, some sources give credit to Arabia for the zero. These numerals later arrived
in Europe by way of Spain and were developed into the system we use and that is used in
most parts of the world today.

beginning of our numerals — O — meaning no-thing — possibly from 7 stars in Big Dipper Constellation — beginnings of 6, 8 & 9 unknown

HINDU-ARABIC NUMERALS 0 0 1 1 2 2 3 3 4 4 5 5 6 6 7 7 8 8 9 9   or 4

use large numerals when writing with all large caps

use small numerals with lower-case and caps and for math   0 1 2 3 4 5 6 7 8 9

HINDU-ARABIC NUMERALS, A.D. 700

ROMAN NUMERALS I II III IV V VI VII VIII IX X XI XII
5-1=4   5   5+1=6   10-1=9   10   10+1=11

Roman Numerals are written vertically with no slope

XX L C D M · MCMLXXXVIII
10+10=20 50 100 500 1,000   How would we write this?*

5mm

* Write your answer here: _____

Address   *11456 N.W. Lakeview Drive*

Note use of small numerals and small caps.   *Portland* OR *97238-1027*

Trace & copy lines above.

Write your own address,

and city, state & zip:

Phone no., abbr. date, height or length.   *(123) 456-7890*   *3/20/94*   *5'7"*

    area code   prefix   number

Money amounts and metric system abbreviations.   *$15.27*   *98¢*   *6 cm*   *124kg*   *539km*

    centimeters   kilograms   kilometers

Time and temperature. Usually we write them with small numerals, but write these large. Which do you prefer?   *8:30 a.m.*   *12:45 p.m.*   *74°F*   *30°C*

    ante meridian - before noon   post meridian - after noon

Fractions   *½ 4⅔ 8¾ 7⅞ 1¹⁵⁄₁₆*

Punctuation. Punctuation aids meaning & expression to written words.   . , : ; ? ! " " — -

    apos-trophe   hyphen   dash

Punctuation and other symbols   ( ) ¢ $ or $ * / (& & &

    parentheses   asterisk   slant or slash

· EGYPTIAN WRITING ·
3,000 BC – AD 400

Of the three kinds of ancient writing scripts used in Egypt, hieroglyphic is the oldest.* ("hieroglyphic" – sacred engraved writing)

At first, they used only pictograms, then idea pictures - ideograms. Finally they used these to spell words.** Egyptians wrote both horizontally ⇋ and vertically.↓

CARTOUCHE OF CLEOPATRA

TRANSLATION: K L E O P A T R A   divine female

Above, you can see that all but two symbols were used to spell Cleopatra. The other two symbols are ideograms.

The Egyptians continued to mix their systems rather than using a single system. (At times we also use more than one system: EXIT)

CARTOUCHE OF TUTANKHAMUN

A cartouche represents a looped rope indicating the king was ruler of all that the sun encircled.

---

* Only one is mentioned here.

** These then became phonograms. (A phonogram is a symbol that stands for a single speech sound. The Egyptians developed the acrophonic principle, see page 83.)

21

If this book is your first experience writing italic, continue to trace the models before copying.

We use the 26 letters of our alphabet

W

daily in reading and writing, but seldom

d

are we aware of their beginnings.

The body height is now 1mm less (4mm) than on previous pages.

The word ALPHABET

²fr ³fi

You may connect fr and fi.

comes from the Greek

names of the first two

letters of their alpha-

bet, ALPHA and BETA.

Some time before 1,300 B.C., the Phoeni-

s

cian alphabet was brought to Greece.

The Greeks added vowels to the alphabet.

4mm

· THE PHOENICIAN ALPHABET ·
about 2,000 BC

Many historians feel we can thank the Phoenicians for the beginning of our alphabet. It is thought that their alphabet of 22 letters* was developed from Egyptian hieroglyphs. The Phoenicians used all of their symbols as consonants.

A	B	C and G	D	E	F, V and Y	H
I	J came later, as did U and W	K	L	M	N	O
P	Q	R	S	T	X	Z

Can you translate this?**

All of those who came in touch with the Phoenicians borrowed their alphabet and changed it to suit their own needs.

SELF-EVALUATION: Are you beginning ā d̄ ḡ q̄ c̄ s̄ with a horizontal line?
Are you ending b p with a horizontal line?

* ⊕ (th) and ₶ (ts) complete the 22 symbols.
** The Phoenicians wrote from right to left.

The Greeks also helped determine the direction of our writing. The Phoenicians generally wrote from right to left, and early Greek writing followed this same pattern.

ft

You may cross ft and tt in one stroke. It's faster!

tt

Then the Greeks began writing in both directions as the oxen plowed the fields.*
By the 5th century B.C. they had changed to our present way, from left to right.

· GREEK WRITING ·

The Greeks cut letters in stone, scratched letters in clay, wrote on papyrus and on slabs of wood and ivory coated with wax that was stained black. A metal or bone stylus was used to inscribe letters on the wax tablets.

ΑΚΑΔΗΜΙΑ
(ACADEMY)
ΣΧΟΛΗ
(SCHOOL)
ΠΟΙΗΤΗΣ
(POET)

wax tablet   stylus

Boustrophedon Writing*

SOMEGREEKWRITINGWASWRI
TTENASTHEOXENPLOWEDTHE
LANDMANYLETTERSHADTOB
EREVERSEDASIHAVEDONEHER
EANDTHEGREEKSALSOWROTEL
IKETHISWITHOUTSPACESBET
WEENWORDSANDWITHOUT
ANYPUNCTUATIONMARKS

SELF-EVALUATION: Are you leaving about the width of n between words? tonthe

* boustrophedon (büs´-trə-fē´-dən): "ox-turning"

23

Use basic italic for maps, signs, posters, banners – any time you want something easily read at a distance.

Our Writing Heritage

A NOTE:
All the writing in this book, including this map, was done by hand.

The ≈≈≈ waves were purchased, cut carefully to fit the outline, peeled off a large sheet and applied to the outlined map. They are self-sticking.

ATLANTIC OCEAN

Romans *

Etruscans

Rome

Greeks *

BLACK SEA

Constantinople

Athens

MEDITERRANEAN SEA

EUPHRATES RIVER

TIGRIS RIVER

Phoenicians

Sumerians

Egyptians

NILE RIVER

KEY
— lowercase and caps – cities
— ALL CAPS – RIVERS
— some cultures that developed written communication
≈≈≈ BODIES OF WATER

* At different times, the Greeks and the Romans influenced much of the area shown on this map.

WRITING LINES: Lines on pages 93 and 94 are similar to this page. You may reproduce any of the lines (from pages 87 to 96). Use them as a liner sheet under your writing paper or write directly on them. Choose the writing size which is most comfortable for you — 5mm, 4mm, or 3mm.

On this page, the base lines 1–14 are spaced similarly to wide ruled notebook paper:

by
they
the

1 The Etruscans acquired the alphabet
2 from the Greeks. In turn, the alphabet
3 was further developed by the Romans.
4
5
6
7

College ruled:

by
they
the

8 Today we use
9 all 23 of the
10 Roman letters. **
11
12
13
14

· THE ETRUSCANS ·
1,000 B.C.–200 B.C.

ꟿ𐌘Ꚛ Ⴟ𐌕𐌘𐌐Ϻ𐌋𐌏Ꞷ𐌁𐌋𐌇𐌊𐌉⊗𐌁𐌉Ↄ𐌃𐌁ꟿ

(The Etruscans apparently came from Asia Minor to Italy and borrowed the Greek alphabet. This tablet shows an early form of the Etruscan alphabet. They remain a people of mystery since no one as yet has been able to translate their writings.)

This is a sketch of an 8th century B.C. Etruscan writing tablet. It is called the MARSILIANA ABECEDARIUM.

** The letters j, u and w were added later.

SELF-EVALUATION: Are your letters close together within words? Trace the models for help.

HANDWRITING TIPS

To alleviate pinching your writing tool, tap your finger three times. The way your finger rests on the tool is the way you should hold it as you write. Tap periodically!

•

Note that this is handwriting—not finger or arm writing. Move from the wrist with minimal finger movement. Write an "m" arcade and a "u" arcade for practice:

arch mmm mmm mmm mmm
counter

uuuu uuuu uuuu uuuu

Write these arcades quickly in a relaxed manner. Practicing the arcade in spare moments—as you wait for an appointment, as you talk on the phone—will help you gain rhythm in your writing.

•

The cursive handwriting many of us learned in school has loops in ascenders and descenders that often cause illegibility.

fill *fill*
hill *hill*

looped cursive   cursive italic

As you learn cursive italic, begin eliminating the loops in the ascenders and descenders of your own handwriting if you currently use them.

We read letters from the top— can you read these two words?

AMERICA

VICTORIA

We read the tops of lower-case letters at the waist line area. Italic letters are easily read because they are loop free.

•

Check the interior and exterior counters of families 5 and 6:

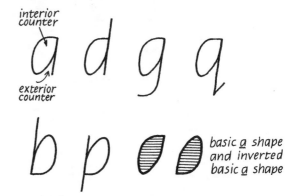

interior counter

exterior counter

a d g q

b p

basic *a* shape and inverted basic *a* shape

NOTE: The basic *a* shape and the inverted basic *a* shape have identical counters as do the arch: n and the inverted arch: u

Maintaining consistent counters of these letters will help you achieve a harmonious rhythmic hand. Practice the following words:

adage   bundle

pique   pod

NOTE: Invert (rotate) "pod." Are counters consistent?

•

Establish your own waist line when using notebook paper. A consistent body height (x height) is one of the essential characteristics of legibility. (See SIZE GUIDE, p.54)

HANDWRITING TIPS, continued

Look carefully at the letter shapes. It's very easy to say, "I know the shape of A — I've written it all my life." However, you may have overlooked the actual shape of the letter A.

Ways to improve your ability to see shapes: First, look at the negative spaces—the counters of the letters. Draw only the counter shapes and you'll see letters in a new way, for example:

Second, look at letter shapes upside down. It may be exasperating to read, but it is an ideal way to see the shapes of letters.

umop apis dn buḷꓕᴉɹʍpuɐɥ umo ɹnoⱯ ʇⱯ ʞooꓶ

"In copying signatures, forgers turn the originals upside down to see the exact shapes of the letters more clearly."[1]

•

Let the speed of your writing suit the task, but don't sacrifice legibility for speed. You and others must be able to read it.

•

ONE WAY TO PRACTICE:

1. Trace model.
2. Write letter 3 times.
3. Compare your letter with model.
   Check: a. letter slope
             b. letter width
             c. letter counter
4. Retrace model.
5. Adjust your letter as needed.
6. Rewrite letter alternating with another letter.
7. Evaluate your writing.
8. Close your eyes and write the letter.

P A T I E N C E

•

If you write a backhand with letters sloping to the left, you can change your letter slope by shifting your paper. There is no need to alter the way you hold your writing tool. It is generally easier to read letters that are vertical or that slope to the right. Whether you are left-handed or righthanded, experiment with paper position.

•

After you complete WRITE NOW, use italic for all of your handwriting at home and at work. As you journey through this book, begin addressing envelopes for practice. Then start writing letters to friends. Many of us feel we have little time to write letters, but it is a wonderful way to practice your italic and also keep in touch with friends. And once in a-while at the end of a busy day, you may return home and find a reply in your own mailbox.

•

1. Betty Edwards. DRAWING ON THE RIGHT SIDE OF THE BRAIN. Los Angeles: J. P. Tarcher, Inc., 1979, p. 51.

PART TWO

Cursive Italic

Transition to Cursive Lower-case
Capitals
Eight Joins
Writing Practice
Timed Writings
Adaptations
Guidelines
Samples

TRANSITION TO CURSIVE LOWER-CASE

Serifs are lines added to the main strokes of a letter. Some serifs are slightly rounded and some are sharp. Serifs are used in cursive italic.

slightly rounded entrance serif · sharp serif

n exit serif · *p*

n becomes *n* · *d* becomes *d* · *j* becomes *j* jot↗

entrance and exit serifs added · exit serif added · sharp entrance serif

CURSIVE LOWER-CASE	a b c d e f g h i j k l m n o p q r s t u v w x y z*

serif (sĕr´if): a fine line added to a letter

ENTRANCE SERIFS
1. m   n   r   x

Roll into m, n, r, x.
2. m   n   r   x

When joining, keep diagonal straight.
3. mn   nn   nr   nx

EXIT SERIFS
4. a   d   h   i (´ or ·)   k

Roll out of a, d, h, i, k, l, m, n, u & z.
5. a   d   h   i   k

When joining, serifs are like hands reaching out to join letters.
6. an   dn   hn   in   kn

7. l   m   n   u   z

8. i   m   n   u   z

When joining, keep diagonal straight.
9. ln   mn   nn   un   zn

SHARP ENTRANCE SERIFS
10. j (´ or ·)   p   v   w

Angle into j, p, v, & w.
11. j   p   v   w

When joining, diagonal (serif) extends to center then swings up.
12. nj   np

13. nv   nw

JOTTED i, j DESCENDER f
i (↗ jot ´ or · dot)   i   j   j   ff

· ROMAN WRITING ·

A gold brooch, the *PRAENESTE FIBULA*, 7th century B.C., contains the earliest known Latin inscription. It was found about 20 miles southeast of Rome.

Early Roman letterforms began with Latin inscriptions in stone and on metal. They also wrote on papyrus, wax tablets, bark & pottery. Their early letters resembled Greek & Etruscan as shown above. Later they became the capital letters we still use today.

* ibcegoqsty Remain the same.

CURSIVE CAPITALS

The Roman alphabet is derived from the Phoenician alphabet to which the Greeks added vowels. Phoenician evolved from Egyptian hieroglyphs.

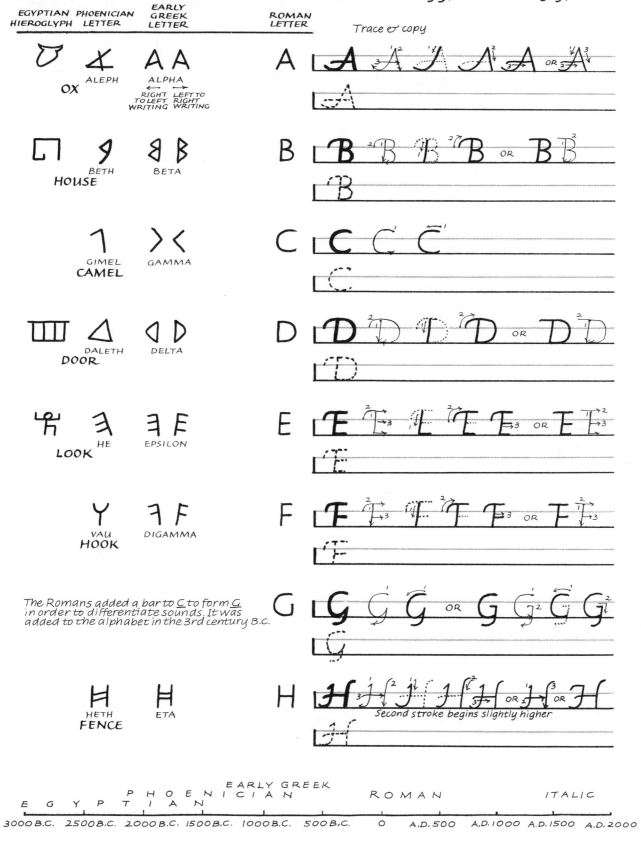

EGYPTIAN HIEROGLYPH	PHOENICIAN LETTER	EARLY GREEK LETTER	ROMAN LETTER	Trace & copy

The Romans added a bar to C to form G in order to differentiate sounds. It was added to the alphabet in the 3rd century B.C.

Second stroke begins slightly higher

OX — ALEPH — ALPHA — RIGHT TO LEFT WRITING — LEFT TO RIGHT WRITING — A

HOUSE — BETH — BETA — B

GIMEL CAMEL — GAMMA — C

DOOR — DALETH — DELTA — D

LOOK — HE — EPSILON — E

VAU HOOK — DIGAMMA — F

G

HETH FENCE — ETA — H

EARLY GREEK
PHOENICIAN
EGYPTIAN   ROMAN   ITALIC

| 3000 B.C. | 2500 B.C. | 2000 B.C. | 1500 B.C. | 1000 B.C. | 500 B.C. | 0 | A.D. 500 | A.D. 1000 | A.D. 1500 | A.D. 2000 |

CURSIVE ITALIC

EGYPTIAN HIEROGLYPH	PHOENICIAN LETTER	EARLY GREEK LETTER	ROMAN LETTER

HAND — YOD — IOTA — I

J is originally a variant of the letter I (long i). It was formally added to the alphabet in the 16th century distinguished from the letter I.

J

PALM — KAPH — KAPPA — K

OX-GOAD — LAMED — LAMBDA — L

WATER — MEM — MU — M

FISH — NUN — NU — N

third stroke begins slightly higher

EYE — AYIN — OMICRON — O

MOUTH — PE — PI — P

QOPH KNOT — KOPPA — Q

Egyptian hieroglyphs are written from top to bottom, usually right to left; also horizontally.

Phoenician letters are written horizontally, right to left, as is Hebrew today.

Early Greek and Early Roman letters are written in alternating directions — right to left, then left to right — boustrophēdon "ox turning" (as a field is plowed). See page 19. After c. 500 B.C., the writing direction left to right is established.

EGYPTIAN HIEROGLYPH	PHOENICIAN LETTER	EARLY GREEK LETTER		ROMAN LETTER	

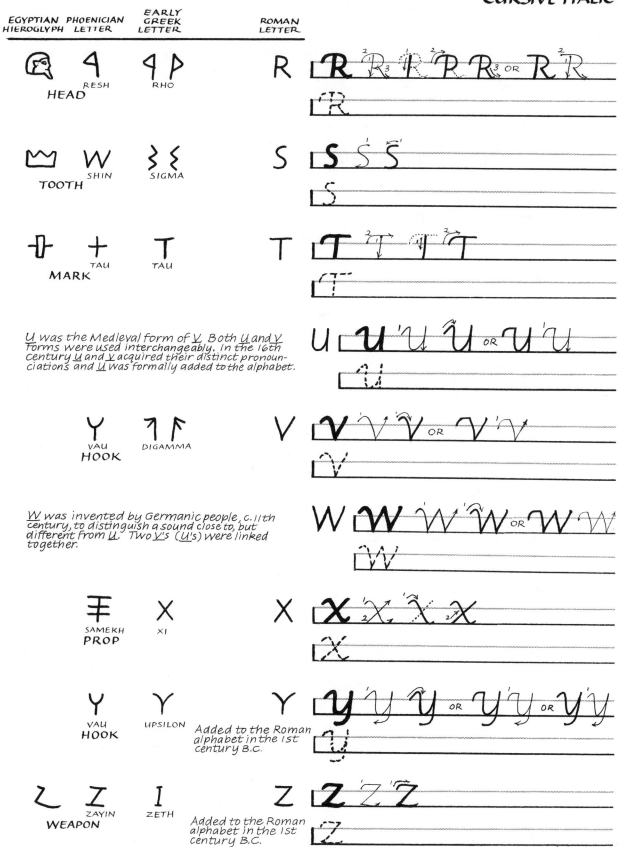

HEAD — RESH — RHO — R

TOOTH — SHIN — SIGMA — S

MARK — TAU — TAU — T

U was the Medieval form of V. Both U and V forms were used interchangeably. In the 16th century U and V acquired their distinct pronounciations and U was formally added to the alphabet.

HOOK VAU — DIGAMMA — V

W was invented by Germanic people, c. 11th century, to distinguish a sound close to, but different from U. Two V's (U's) were linked together.

PROP SAMEKH — XI — X

HOOK VAU — UPSILON — Y

Added to the Roman alphabet in the 1st century B.C.

WEAPON ZAYIN — ZETH — Z

Added to the Roman alphabet in the 1st century B.C.

The development of the alphabet as shown is based on ANCIENT WRITING AND ITS INFLUENCE by Berthold Louis Ullman (1969 M.I.T. Press).

See pages 76-83 for more information about the development of capitals & lower-case.

BASIC AND CURSIVE CAPITALS WITH CURSIVE LOWER-CASE

The height of capitals is 1½ times the body height of lower-case letters.

A A a   A A a   B B b   B B b   C C c   C c

D D d   D D d   E E e   E e or e

F F f   F F f   G G g   G g or G G

H H h   H h H h   I or I I i   I i i or y

J J j   J j j j or y   K K k   K k K k

L L L or L   M M m   M M m

Some capitals are the same for basic & cursive: C, O, Q & S.

N N n   N N n   O O o   O o or O

P P p   P p   Q Q q   O Q q or O Q

R R r   R R r   S S s   S s   T T t   T t t

U U u   U u   V V v   v v   W W w   W w

OPTION: You may prefer to flourish less on capitals: B, D, E, F, P, R or R, T

X X x   X x   X x   Y Y y   Y y   Z Z z   Z z

OPTION: You may prefer to use basic capitals with cursive italic lower-case: *Ann Bill Carlos Dana Ellen Fay Greg*

JOIN 1 *an am ar ax* DIAGONAL · ROLL OVER
Join with a straight diagonal line, then roll over into n,m,r,x.

an | an cn dn en hn in kn ln mn

Trace & copy line above. | an

nn un zn · Ian Jan Len Ann

am | am em im mm nm um · Sam

am

ar | ar cr dr er ir kr ur

ar

ax | ax ex ix ux · Max

ax

Van Dan Kim Pam

· PAPYRUS ·

diameter often 20-30 millimeters

rind removed

inner pith sliced into thin strips

Reeds often grow up to a height of 8 meters.

After the stalks are cut, the thin strips are laid crosswise on a flat surface in a double layer. A cloth is laid over the strips and the papyrus is beaten with a wooden mallet until the strips are matted together.

NOTE: For an alternate join into n, m, r and x see page 35. | Cam Tim Sara

SELF · EVALUATION: Are you joining with a straight diagonal line? *an* (Avoid *an*)

Join 1 is used here. Dotted lines indicate Joins 2-8. | The Egyptians, Greeks, and Romans used papyrus as a writing surface.

The word "paper" is derived from "papyrus."

4mm

JOIN 2

au ay ai at aj ap av aw
al ah ab ak DIAGONAL·SWING UP
Join with a diagonal line blending into a swing-up stroke.

au ay

1. au ay cu cy du dy eu ey hu hy iu iy

Trace & copy line above.
2. au

3. ki ky lu ly mu my nu ny uy zu zy

ai at

5. ai at ci ct di dt ei et hi ht it ki kt li

6. ai

7. lt mi mt ni nt ui ut zi · Pat Mimi

aj ap

9. aj ap ej ep ip lp mp np up · Kip

10. aj

av aw

11. av aw ev ew iv iw uv uw · Lew Liv

12. av

OPTION: You may prefer to round slightly the point of v and points of w at the baseline.

13. av aw ev ew iv iw Lew Liv

14. av

al ah

15. al ah cl ch dl el eh il ih ll ml nl nh

16. al

17. ul uh · Sally Philip Emily Anh Vinh

18.

19.

4mm

ab ak | ab ak ck eb ek ib ik lk nk ub uk · Tab
2 ab

SELF-EVALUATION: Are your joins and letters blending halfway? abt (Avoid) (aw)

Are you joining into l, h, b, e, k with a single line? al (Avoid scoop and loop) (al)

Joins 1-2 are used here. Dotted lines indicate Joins 3-8.

3 The Latin word for
4 scroll is "volumen" from
5 which comes our word
6 "volume."
7
8
9

·SCROLL·
A label (Latin "titulus") is attached to the end for identification.

Some scrolls are more than thirty meters in length.

Both papyrus & parchment are used in scrolls & codices.

·CODEX·
Sheets are folded for easier storage and transporting.

The word "parchment" is from the Latin "pergamena"—from the city Pergamum in Greece. The earliest Greek parchment manuscripts date from the second century B.C.

10 Parchment, made from the skins of
11 animals, was easier to write on than
12 papyrus and soon became the chief
13 writing material. P

Sheep, goat, & calf skins are used for parchment.

14
15
16

OPTION: You may prefer to join into n, m, r, & x with JOIN 2. an am ar ax

an | 17 an en in un · am em im um · Jan Jim
18 an

[Options are shown in broken-line boxes.]

19 ar er ir ur · Sara · ax ex ix ux · Max
20

4mm

JOIN 3 *ao* *as* DIAGONAL · START BACK
Join with a straight diagonal line, then start back into o, s.

ao | ao co do eo ho io ko lo mo no uo zo
ao

as | as cs ds es hs is ks ls ms ns us zs
as

OPTION: You may prefer to keep the top on s when joining: a/s See JOIN 8, page 42.

The top of s is left off in this join. See option.

Leo Julio Luís · L

SELF-EVALUATION: Are you joining with a straight diagonal? *ao* (Avoid *ao*)

Joins 1-3 are used here. Dotted lines indicate Joins 4-8

Paper was invented by the Chinese
in A.D. 105. P

OPTION: You may prefer to use a 2-stroke e. e e
If so, use JOIN 3. Join into the top of e. ae ae
Follow back out of 2nd stroke. en (Avoid en, en)

ae | ae ae ce de he ie ke le me ne ue ze
ae ae

en | en eu el eo ee ea · Len Leo Lee Bea
en

See OPTIONS page 57.

Shelley

Alex

· ORIENTAL PAPERMAKING ·
There are eight major steps in the hand papermaking process as practiced since 610 A.D.

Prints from KAMISUKI CHOHOKI, 1798

branches cut and bundled

outer bark removed

wood steamed

JOIN4 *ae* DIAGONAL INTO E
Join with a diagonal line into e.

---

ae | ae ce de ee he ie ke le me ne ue ze

ae

Mae Lee Julie Katie June Sue

Alex Theo Zeke Shelley Renée

SELF-EVALUATION: Is your join into e a straight diagonal line? *ae*
Does your join into e intersect
the letter at the center? center→ *ae* (Avoid *ae*)

Joins 1-4 are used here. Dotted lines indicate Joins 5-8.

"Ts'ai Lun conceived the idea of
making paper from the bark of trees,
discarded cloth and hemp well-
prepared."

This was written by an ancient Chinese scholar about Ts'ai Lun, a privy councilor to the Royal Court of Ho Ti (89-105 A.D.).

white bark separated from core and washed   bark beaten and beaten still more into pulp   mould dipped in vat filled with pulp & water

JOIN 5 — o̅n t̅n f̅n v̅n w̅n x̅n **HORIZONTAL**
(o̅u o̅o o̅a o̅z o̅t o̅l *These variations are also used with t, f, v, w and x.*)
Join with a horizontal line into all letters except f.

on
on om or ox · o̅u oy oi oj op ov ow
o̅n
o̅o o̅a oc od og oq os o̅z o̅t o̅l oh ob ok

Hoa Thor Joy John Lois Solomon

tn
t̅n tr t̅u ty ti tw t̅o t̅a ts t̅z t̅l th
t̅n
The advantage of joining from the crossbar: there is no need to return to cross the t.
t̅t t̅t Scott Otto Patty Matthew
Double t

OPTION: You may prefer to join out of the first stroke of t (from the base line), then add the crossbar after the word is written.

tn
tn tn tr tu ty ti tl th to ts te ta
tn

NOTE: In this book t is joined into e in this way.

te
te · Pete Kate Nate

OPTION: You may prefer to join out of t into e with a horizontal join.
tc
See page 39 for other options.

te

fn
fn fr fu fy fi fj fo fa fs · ft ft or ft ft · fl
fn

ff ff ff · Jeff Cliff Clifton

It is suggested to lift before e after f.
OPTION: You may prefer to join out of f into e with a horizontal join.
fe

vn	vn vr · vu vy vi · vo · va vs · vt vl ·Aviva

vn.

wn	wn wr · wu wy wi · wo · wa ws · wt wl

wn.

wh wk · Lewis Edwin Newton

xn	xn · xu xy xi · xo xa x.s · xt · xl

Alexis Maxine

SELF-EVALUATION: Are you joining with a straight, horizontal line? ON (^Avoid on)

Joins 1–5 are used here. Dotted lines indicate Joins 6–8.

Hand papermaking processes today use plant fibers or rag pulp.

H

NOTE: Join into e out of o, v, w, and x with a modified join. **OPTION:** oe

oe	oe ve we xe · Joe Eve Gwen Axel

oe

OPTION: You may prefer to lift before e after o, v, w, x, and t.

oe	oe te fe ve we xe · Joe Eve Peter

or Peter (see p.38)

oe

OPTION: You may prefer to use a 2-stroke e after o, t, f, v, w, and x.

oe	oe te fe ve we xe · Joe Eve Peter

oe

JOING *rn ru ro ra re* DIAGONAL OUT OF R
Join with a short diagonal line into all letters except f.

| rn | *rn rm rr · Arne Carmen Larry* |

rn (2)

| ru | *ru ry ri rt rv rl rh rb rk · Art* |

ru (4)

| ro ra | *ro · ra rc rd rs · Arturo Sara Cars* |

ro (6)

| re | *re · Karen Greta* | **OPTION:** If you prefer a 2-stroke e, join into the top of e. | *re Karen* |

re (8)   *re re* (2)

SELF-EVALUATION: Are you joining out of <u>r</u> just below the waist line?
Are you bending the top of <u>r</u> at the waist line?

waist line ↓ (Avoid)
rn (*m*)
<u>rn</u> can look like <u>m</u> or <u>vn</u>

Joins 1-6 are used here. Dotted lines indicate Joins 7-8.

Hand papermak- (9,10)
ing mills use this (11)
process today. (12)

(13)

(14)

· WESTERN PAPERMAKING ·

Deckle frame fits tightly over the mould
Mould Woven brass wires are attached to frame

Vat of pulpe water

Cotton or linen rags are beaten in water to form the pulp. The mould and the deckle are immersed in the vat of pulp. A thin layer of pulp is gathered on the mould.

SIDE VIEW pulp → deckle → mould

The deckle is removed and the mould with the layer of pulp is turned over and rolled onto a piece of felt

pulp placed on felt

After being pressed, dried, and sized, a piece of paper is ready to write on.

OPTION: You may prefer to point the top of <u>r</u> to aid legibility. *rn*

| rn | *rn ru ro re · Sara* | (15)

rn (16)

OPTION: You may prefer to lift after <u>r</u> to aid legibility.

| ru | *ru ro ra re · Karen · ru* | (17)

4mm

If you prefer to lift after <u>r</u>, keep letters close together.

JOIN 7 — *sn bn pn* HORIZONTAL TO DIAGONAL

Join with a horizontal line blending into a diagonal line into all letters except f.

---

sn

1. sn sm sr *or* sn sm sr · su sy si st sp sv
2. sn
3. sw sl sh sb sk · so ss *or* ss · se · sa sc sd sg
4.
5. Jessie José Justin J

bn

6. bn br *or* bn br · bu by bi bt bl bb · bo bs
7. bn
8. be · ba bc bd bg · Pablo Bobby Deborah
9.

pn

10. pn pr *or* pn pr · pu py pi pt pp pl ph · po
11. pn
12. ps *or* ps · pe · pa pc pd pg · Hope Joseph
13.

SELF-EVALUATION: Are you following back out of s, b, & p? sr br pr (Avoid br pr)

Joins 1–7 are used here. Dotted lines indicate Join 8.

14. Wood is the basic raw material from
15. which most machine made paper is
16. manufactured. W

Some machine-made papers are made with 100% wood fiber, some 100% cotton rag, and some are mixtures.

17.
18.

OPTION: You may prefer to lift after b and p.
If so, be sure the next letter follows closely. br pr bo po

JOIN 8 · aa ac ad ag aq as · DIAGONAL TO HORIZONTAL

Join with a diagonal line blending into the horizontal beginning strokes of a, c, d, g, q, and s.

aa ad
1. aa ad ca ea ed da dd ha ia id ka
2. aa
3. la ld ma na nd ua ud za · Shalonda
4.

ag aq
5. ag aq eg eq ig iq ng ug uq · Quang
6. ag

ac
7. ac cc ec ic uc · Vic Alice Michael
8. ac

as
9. as cs ds es hs is ks ls ms ns us zs
10. as

Joins 7 & 8
11. sa sc ss · ba · pa ps · Lissa Barbara
12. sa

SELF-EVALUATION: Are your a, c, d, g, q and s flat on top? aa (Avoid aa or aa)
(horizontal at the waistline)

All joins are used here.
13. Our word "pen" is from
14. the Latin word for
15. feather—"penna."
16.
17.
18.

· PENS ·

The first pens were cut from reeds.

Later, flight feathers of geese or swans were used.

Quills were the primary pen used for writing on parchment and paper until the 19th century.

LIFTS (NO JOIN) — *af az · ga ja qu ya*

Lift writing tool before f & z and after g, j, q & y.

af	Olaf Jeffrey Alfredo Alfreda

az	Alonzo Lizzie Kazuaki Elizabeth

Lift before z from the base line.

ga ja	Inga Bridget Helge Elijah Sonja

qu ya	Jacqueline Joyce Beryl Lloyd Sylvia

Joins are natural spacers. When letters in a word are not joined, be sure they are close together.   af az ga ja qu ya

NOTE: You may prefer to join out of g, y, q, and y: *go jo qu yo*   *Speed may alter the shape of descenders so they are straighter, longer or more curved.*

We read letters from the top (see page 25). For the sake of legibility do not add loops to ascenders. Addition of loops to descenders does not hamper legibility if adequate space is left between lines of writing.

j y q g y j

REVIEW	1 am am ar ax (an am ar ax) ·

Options in parenthesis.

2 au ay ai at aj ap av aw al ah ab ak · 3 ao as

(aea) · 4 ae · 5 on tn (tn) fn vn wn xn ·

6 rn (rn) · 7 sn bn pn · 8 aa ac ad ag aq as

A quick brown fox jumps over the lazy dog.

4mm

WRITING PRACTICE

SENATVS·PO
IMP·CAESARI·
TRAIANO·AV(
MAXIMO·TRIB

The Trajan Inscription·Roman Forum
112-113 A.D. *Cast made by Edward Catich*
(small portion shown)
From THE ROMAN LETTER by James Hayes

The actual
height of S
(top left)
is 4⅝".

The Roman inscrip-
tional letters* serve as
the models for our
capitals.

* Note the
exception to
the horizontal
join out of t.
The join from
t to a one-
stroke e is
from the
baseline.

te

Other options:
te tt te
See page 38.

They were written* with a brush, then
incised in the stone and painted.

Square Capitals were derived from
the large inscriptional letters.

They were written with a reed pen on
parchment and used as a bookhand
from the first to the fifth centuries.

SQUARE
CAPITALS

ABCDEFGHIKLMNOPQRSTVXYZ

After Virgil manuscript - 4th century   *The 23 letters   of the Roman alphabet.*

RUSTIC CAPITALS

ΛBCDEFGHIKLMNOPQRSTUXYZ

After Virgil manuscript 4th-5th century.

Rustics were written with a reed pen on papyrus and parchment.

The flowing, narrow letters of Rustics show the influence of speed and the need to conserve materials. This script was used mainly for special editions of poetry. T

The name Uncial comes from St. Jerome - meaning "inch high".

Uncial writing was used primarily for copies of the Bible. The curving forms show the desire to make letters with the fewest possible strokes. Uncial was used from the third century to the tenth century. U

We see in Uncial the beginning of our lower-case letters:

λ → a, α
δ → d
e → e
h → h
m → m
q → q

UNCIAL

ABCDEFGhIKLMNOPQRSTUXYZ

After Gospels of St. Gall - 5th-6th century

abcdefghiklmnopqrſtuxy&z

CAROLINGIAN

(long s)

In the 9th century, an increased interest in culture led to the copying of the Latin classics. This led to the advancement of writing.

The Carolingian script was used for copying large quantities of Latin manuscripts. In use from 800 to 1200, these letters have lengthened ascenders and descenders.

At its best, Gothic is beautiful but hard to read.

The Gothic script is the bookhand of the late Middle Ages. Its angular letters show the need to save space.

uite often large letters appear at the beginning of paragraphs.

This Q is from a manuscript written by Claricia, a nun c.1200. She represents herself as the tail of the Q. (From WOMEN ARTISTS by K. Peterson and J. Wilson.)

abcdefghiklmnopqrstuxyz GOTHIC

Around the 13th century, a faint slash was added to i to aid legibility.

ROTUNDA (Round Gothic) **abcdefghiklmnopqrstuvxyz**

15TH CENTURY BOOKHAND
(HUMANIST BOOKHAND)

abcdefghiklmnopqrſstuxy&z·jvw
(long s)

The scholars collected classical texts—many written in Carolingian. Their Gothic hand (Rotunda) was influenced by the elegant Carolingian to create 15th century Bookhand.

A clear, legible bookhand was developed during the Renaissance by Italian scholar-scribes in the fourteenth & fifteenth centuries. It is the basis of many typefaces.

The transition from bookhand to cursive is:
1) round to elliptical forms
O to O
2) vertical to slightly sloped
on to on
3) unjoined to joined.
iu to iu

Italic, a cursive form of this book-hand, flourished for two hundred years as the basic script for business and correspondence. Today it continues as a practical handwriting.

ITALIC

Anonymous scribe 1490

(The Houghton Library, Harvard University, Department of Printing and Graphic Arts) Reproduced by permission.

altior ordo sacerdotalis · Stephanus qq: papa secundus Romanum imperium in personam magnifici Caroli á Grecis transtulit in Germanos. Alius uti Ro

4mm

Seguita lo essempio delle lre che pono
ligarsi con tutte le sue seguenti, in tal mo-
do cioe

aa ab ac ad ae af ag ah ai ak al am an
ao ap aq ar as af at au ax ay az
Il medesmo farai con d i k l m n u.
Le ligature poi de c f s ſt sonno
le infra-

scritte

ct, fa ff fi fm fn fo fr fu fy,
ſt ſt

ſſ ſſ ß ſt, ta te ti tm tn to tg tr tt tu
tx ty
Con le restanti littere de lo Alphabeto, che
sono, b e g h o p q r x y z z
non si deue ligar mai lra
alcuna seguente

ITALIC

The first instruction
manual of the italic
script was LA OPERINA
by Arrighi, printed in
Rome in 1522.

LA OPERINA, Ludovico degli Arrighi, Italy, 1522
THE FIRST WRITING BOOK by John Howard Benson
(Yale University Press, 1954). Reproduced by permission.

Letters above
are angular as
they were cut
and printed
from woodblocks.

In Italy, italic served as a personal
hand for many, including Raphael,
Michelangelo, and Cellini.

Writing on
pages 48-49
offers practice
using the base
line only—
similar to
notebook
paper spacing.
(See page 54)

NOTE: The
2-stroke *e*
is used in this
paragraph.
(see OPTION
page 36)

In England this script became
known as the "italique hande." Italic
was the hand of courtiers, secretaries,
and royalty.

ROUND HAND
THE UNIVERSAL PENMAN
by George Bickham
(Dover Publications, Inc.,
New York)
LETTERING: MODES OF WRITING
IN WESTERN EUROPE FROM
ANTIQUITY TO THE END OF THE
18TH CENTURY by Hermann
Degering (Taplinger/Pentalic,
1978). Reproduced by permission.

abbcddefoghhiijkkllllmnnoppqrsfstuvwxyz.
ABCDEFGHIJKLMMM
NNOP2RSTUVWXXYYZ.

During the 17th to 19th centuries Round hand was written with a flexible nib on paper and with an engraver's burin on copperplate.

Round hand was the result of the addition of ornate flourishes, loops on ascenders & descenders, more pen lifts, and an extreme slope of 38°.

The looped cursive or "commercial cursive" in use today is patterned after Round hand. The loops, extreme slope, and forced joins make looped cursive often illegible when written fast.

"Cursive" comes from the Latin "currere"— to run.

Italic handwriting, with its roots in the Renaissance, provides a handsome, graceful script for today. Both basic italic and cursive italic serve well as a practical, legible handwriting.

Cursive italic maintains its legibility when written quickly.

Italic is a loop free, clean-cut script for the computer age.

To increase writing speed, do timed writing exercises on page 50.

You will develop your own unique, personal hand. See page 51, Adaptations.

Handwriting is a lifelong skill, and good handwriting is a lifelong joy!

Write cursive italic with an edged pen.

See pages 62-74.

TIMED WRITINGS — SPEED Use the timed writings to help increase speed for formal, informal, & rapid writing. See page 55.

Begin by writing the following sentence on another sheet of paper as a warm-up for the timed writings. *If you prefer, substitute another pangram or sentence.*

A quick brown fox jumps over the lazy dog.

I. TIME LENGTH: 1 MINUTE Write the sentence at your most comfortable speed. If you finish before the time is up, begin the sentence again.

_____

_____

| BOX 1 | _____ |

Count the number of words written and write the number in Box 1.

2. TIME LENGTH: 1 MINUTE Write sentence a little faster. *Try to add 1 or 2 more words to your total.*

_____

_____

| BOX 2 | _____ |

Write the number of words written in Box 2.

3. TIME LENGTH: 1 MINUTE Write sentence as fast as you can. *Maintain legibility.*

_____

_____

_____

| BOX 3 | _____ |

Write the number of words written in Box 3.

4. TIME LENGTH: 1 MINUTE Write sentence at a comfortable speed.

_____

_____

| BOX 4 | _____ |

Write the number of words written in Box 4.

The goal is to increase the number of words written per minute. Aim for an increase in the total of Box 4 over Box 1. Have you increased by one or more? You can increase speed without sacrificing legibility. Repeat process periodically.

BLIND WRITING *Using the same sentence, do this exercise as a follow-up to the timed writings.* Begin with a non-lined sheet of paper. Close your eyes. Picture in your mind's eye the shape of each letter as you write. *Take all the time you need. You may be amazed how well you can write with your eyes closed.*

ADAPTATIONS Your own personal handwriting style is created by your variations of shape, slope, size, spacing, and speed.

SHAPE Italic is based on an elliptical shape which may be standard O, expanded O, or compressed O. See SHAPE GUIDELINES, page 52.

Standard · a quick brown fox jumps over the lazy dog

Expanded · a quick brown fox jumps over the

Compressed · a quick brown fox jumps over the lazy dog

SLOPE Writing slope may vary from 0° to 15.° Standard is 5.° Whichever slope is preferred, be consistent. See SLOPE GUIDELINES, page 53.

0° · a quick brown fox jumps over the lazy dog.

5° (STANDARD) · a quick brown fox jumps over the lazy dog

10° · a quick brown fox jumps over the lazy dog

15° · a quick brown fox jumps over the lazy dog

SIZE Each of us has a comfortable letter height. See SIZE GUIDELINES, page 54.

4mm · 3mm · 2½mm
a quick brown fox jumps over the lazy dog

SPACING The space between letters in a word & between words may be more expanded or compressed. See SPACING GUIDELINES, page 55.

Expanded spacing · a quick brown fox jumps over the

Compressed spacing · a quick brown fox jumps over the lazy dog

SPEED Let the speed of writing fit the task at hand, maintaining legibility. Notice how speed affects shape, strokes, slope, & spacing. See SPEED, page 55.

Moderate speed · a quick brown fox jumps over the lazy dog

Rapid speed · a quick brown fox jumps over the lazy

STROKE ADAPTATIONS: One or two-stroke e; one or two-stroke k-k; joining out of first or second stroke of t; plus your own innovations. See page 52.

As you progress, your italic handwriting becomes very personal and unique.
See Samples, pages 58-60, 72-74.

SHAPE/STROKES GUIDELINES

The shapes of all lower-case basic italic letters are the same as the corresponding cursive italic letters. All letters are written with a continuous stroke, except the crossed letters f, t, and x and the dotted letters i and j. (Optional two-stroke e and k)

Basic italic lower-case has eight families grouped according to letter shape. Lower-case letters are presented first since we read and write lower-case approximately 98% of the time. (Pages 14-17)

Building on previously learned concepts saves learning time. The transition from basic italic to cursive italic is a natural one, as both use the same shapes and slope. Write the letters unjoined and it's printing (basic italic). Add entrance and exit serifs to basic italic letters—like hands reaching out, then add extensions to join the letters and it's cursive italic. There are eight joins using diagonal and horizontal connections. (Pages 33-43)

an an an an

An easy transition from printed to cursive capital letters is provided. Basic italic capitals are shown in four width groups. (Page 18) Cursive capitals retain the same shape as basic italic with flourishes added. Only the Y changes shape—to Y. (Pages 29-31) The writer may prefer to use basic capitals with cursive lower-case.

OPTIONS: The lower-case letters in this book are modeled after the standard shape. Expanded and compressed are also acceptable.

STANDARD — body height | Width is slightly more than half the body height.

EXPANDED — Width is slightly less than the body height.

COMPRESSED — Width is close to half the body height.

(Also see page 51, shape options.)

Write in the space below using a comfortable letter width. Aim for consistency.

EVALUATE & ADJUST: Using 3-ring notebook paper, place one of the holes over a letter to single out that letter. Compare its width to a similar letter. Are your o's similar in width? All letters are the same width as o, except i, l, and r are narrower, and m and w are wider. Compare the width of o to a different letter to check consistency. Is your general letter width closer to standard, expanded or compressed? Adjust letters as needed.

BASIC ITALIC: All letters start at the top and go down or over. (Except d and e)

CURSIVE ITALIC: Lift before f and z; lift after g, j, q, and y.

SLOPE GUIDELINES

Generally, a natural slope for hand-writing is slightly slanted to the right from the vertical. This book is written with a 5° slope. Cursive is written with the same slope as basic italic; there is no need to change slope.

OPTIONS: Italic allows a choice of slope—from a vertical of 0° to a slope of 15°. Whichever slope is preferred, the goal is to maintain a consistent slope. Choice range:

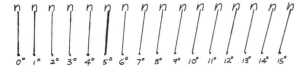

0° 1° 2° 3° 4° 5° 6° 7° 8° 9° 10° 11° 12° 13° 14° 15°

Which is your most comfortable slope? Choose either 5° as used in this book or any other degree between 0° and 15°. (See page 51, slope options.)

Write in the space below using your own natural slope. Aim for consistency.

EVALUATE & ADJUST: Check the consistency of your slope by drawing slope lines through the center of each letter—line up with the downstroke or axis of each letter. When there are varying slopes, one must be chosen. Either choose the slope which appears most often (Example A) or choose the slope in the middle of the range (Example B). Then draw parallel lines next to the slope you have chosen. Now use the parallel lines as your slope guide.

		EXAMPLE A	EXAMPLE B
1.	Write word		
2.	Draw slope lines over letters		
3.	Select one slope		
4.	Draw parallel lines		
5.	Write over slope lines		

OTHER SLOPE OPTIONS: If the writer prefers an extreme slope of more than 15°, it is acceptable as long as legibility is not compromised. An extreme slope can often be adjusted by changing the paper position. (See page 10) An extreme backhand is hard to read. A _slight_ backhand is acceptable. Check paper position.

A SLOPE GUIDE for your personal choice of slope is helpful. Use a sheet of notebook paper positioned at an angle underneath the writing paper so that the lines line up with your chosen slope. Use paper clips or removable tape to hold in place. Outline the edge of the writing paper on the undersheet so it can be easily repositioned under other writing paper.

FOR 0°   FOR 5°   FOR 10°   FOR 15°

(See page 87 for 5° slope lines.)

NOTE: As we write we all vary slightly from our chosen slope. (We are not machines!) An overall, even, balanced writing is our goal.

SIZE GUIDELINES

All letters sit on the base line. The waist line (dotted in this book) indicates the top of the body height—the height of an <u>x</u> or any letter without an ascender or descender. The size of capitals and letters with ascenders or descenders is 1½ times the body height.

The f, having both an ascender and descender in cursive, is 2 times the body height.

This size relationship allows writing lines (base lines) to be close without tangling ascenders & descenders.

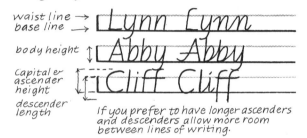

waist line →
base line →
body height ↕
Capital & ascender height ↕
descender length ↕

If you prefer to have longer ascenders and descenders allow more room between lines of writing.

This relationship between the body height and the size of capitals, ascenders, and descenders is similar to many typefaces used in books, typewriters and computers.

This book uses 9mm, 5mm, & 4mm body heights for basic italic and 4mm body height for cursive italic and the edged pen italic.

If a shorter body height is preferred, use 3mm lines on page 95.

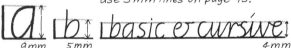

9mm   5mm   4mm

OPTIONS: Each person has a comfortable size of writing. If the body height is too small, legibility is impaired. Consistency of body height is the key to even-looking handwriting—along with even letter shape and slope. Choose your comfortable letter height as you write on the line below. Aim for consistent body height.

EVALUATE & ADJUST: On your writing above, draw a line parallel to the base line touching the top of the body height of most of the letters. This is your natural body height. Does the body height vary? A slight variation is acceptable. If the variation is considerable the writing has an uneven look.

size   size   size
even   acceptable   needs adjusting

To achieve a more even body height, draw a waist line parallel to the base line below using your chosen body height. Write within the lines, aiming for an even consistent size.

Your choice of waist line—draw parallel to this base line.

A SIZE GUIDE for your personal choice of body height is helpful. Take two sheets of notebook paper (see sizes below) and shift one sheet down half a space or whatever body height you choose. Fasten the two sheets with paper clips. The faint line showing through will serve as a waist line. *You may want to trace the lines on your second sheet with a ballpoint or fiber-tip pen to allow you to see through more easily.*

NOTEBOOK PAPER SIZES *(Actual sizes may vary)*

notebook paper   9mm space
wide ruled   4½mm body height

7mm space   *notebook paper*
3¾mm body height   *college ruled*

When writing on notebook paper without a size guide, choose an imaginary waist line to suit your own comfortable size.

54

SPACING GUIDELINES

There are two aspects of spacing. One is the distance between letters within a word and the other is the distance between words within a sentence.

The letters within a word are quite closely written. In basic italic, there are three rules of spacing:

1. two curves are the closest —almost touching;
2. a curve and a downstroke are a little farther apart;
3. two downstrokes are the farthest apart.

pod   home   hill
 1   2   3

"Imagine you have a small measuring glass. It holds just so much water. Now, you have to pour the water out of the glass into the spaces between the letters, and each one has to contain exactly the same amount—whatever its shape." BenShahn

Use the width of an n between words.

In cursive italic, joins are natural spacers. When lifts are advised (before f e r z; after g j q e r y) consideration must be given to even, close spacing. *(Page 43)*

OPTIONS: Standard spacing is used in this book. Expanded and compressed spacing are options.

standard   standard
expanded   expand
compressed   compressed

In the space below write with your most comfortable spacing. Aim for even, balanced writing.

SPEED GUIDELINES

Writing speed is highly individual. After learning all the joins, begin to increase writing speed. Timed writing exercises are on page 50. Do these exercises periodically. Italic generally remains legible when written quickly.

OPTIONS: There are three general speeds of writing:
1. slow speed for learning letter shapes and formal writing
2. moderate speed for everyday informal writing
3. fast speed for note taking and other rapid writing.

Let the speed fit the writing task.

EVALUATE & ADJUST: In any evaluation of writing, legibility is the greatest concern. Can you read it? Adjust your speed to suit the need—both for legibility and the writing task at hand. Speed can be increased without decreasing legibility. An average number of words per minute for moderate speed is 15-30 words and for rapid writing is 31-40 words. Take the time you need—speed is second to your writing enjoyment.

Your own variations of shape, strokes, slope, size, spacing, & speed make your italic handwriting unique—your personal style.

ADVANTAGES OF ITALIC

We are a "please print" nation. We are asked to print on forms, labels, and applications. Businesses often require employees to print or type memos. Handwriting has become a national embarrassment.

Why is this? The answer is simple. The looped cursive handwriting we commonly use in our schools has two major problems.

The first problem is a lack of continuity. As children, most of us learn 52 letter shapes in "ball and stick" style (A a). Then we are required to forget what we have learned and start over with looped cursive—52 completely new shapes written with a different slope. Many find this a frustrating transition, with adverse effects on handwriting that persist into adulthood.

Secondly, the cursive letters are weighted down with loops, curlicues, and long entrance and exit serifs which often mask the letter shape:

$\mathcal{G}$ (Find the G: $\mathcal{G}$)   2 or 2 (Find the Q: 2)

Loops also cause ambiguity in letter identification: $\mathcal{lli}$
Is there an e, i, l, t, or u here?

As adults, many of us abandon looped cursive and either print in all caps or invent our own lower-case printing which often looks very much like italic. Few return to "ball and stick".

Italic avoids these problems. Cursive italic letter shapes and slope are identical to those of basic italic. This saves learning time and reinforces muscle memory of shape and movement. Italic provides clear, loop-free letters.

Italic letterforms are easier for dyslexic writers. There are no mirror image letters which often cause reversals. ("Ball and stick" b-d, p-q)
Dyslexia is an organizing disability which impairs short term memory, perception, and handwriting skills.

Italic offers elliptical shapes suited to natural hand movements. Many adults find italic handwriting satisfying as both a practical, legible form of communication and an aesthetically pleasing script. American Medical News states that, "Busy adults who've taken up italic report that the rewards of writing in this style are so abundant that they are motivated to practice".[1] A TIME article on italic handwriting says, "An improved hand would be a boon to American culture".[2]

"BALL AND STICK"; LOOPED CURSIVE	BASIC ITALIC; CURSIVE ITALIC
A quick brown fox	A quick brown fox
A quick brown fox	A quick brown fox

1. Flora Johnson Skelly. "Grace Under Pressure", American Medical News, February 23, 1990, p.37
2. Wolf Von Eckardt. "Reforming With Zigs and Zags", TIME, March 21, 1983, p.86

OPTIONS

Frequently handwriting is a compromise between the hand and the eye. The hand needs a comfortable mode of writing and the eye requires a handsome, legible script.

WRITE NOW gives you options in letter shape, strokes, slope, size, spacing, and speed. Your hand and eye will choose what feels and looks best.

For example, WRITE NOW offers a two-stroke e as an option to the one-stroke e (see pages 36, 37). If the eye prefers the look of the two-stroke e, then the hand complies and lifts mid-letter. The 16th century scribes used a two-stroke e as do many writers today (see pages 47, 48, 58-60, 72-74).

As adults learning a new handwriting you have many choices. You may prefer to use only the basic italic letterforms, joining if and when it is convenient. You may find elements of italic handwriting you like and use them to modify your current script. Or, you may completely change your handwriting style to italic and turn in a new signature card at the bank. Whatever you choose, your handwriting will be uniquely yours. Your own personality will come shouting through.

Public, private, and home schools are using italic handwriting with great success. The ITALIC HANDWRITING SERIES by the authors of WRITE NOW, provides a complete handwriting program for children from kindergarten through sixth grade.

For information write to:
Portland State University
Continuing Education Press
P.O. Box 1394
Portland, Oregon 97207

Inspiration for this book came from the late Lloyd Reynolds, formerly Professor at Reed College, who said, "There are 71 million students in public and private schools, colleges, and universities. Most of them are frustrated by bad handwriting. I decided that helping them was important. I believe William Morris' statement,

'A true source of human happiness lies in taking a genuine interest in all the details of daily life and elevating them by art'." [1]

William Morris 1834-1896   Lloyd Reynolds 1902-1978

1. Lloyd Reynolds. "Handwriting and Calligraphy", _Oregon Rainbow_, No. 4, 1976   (Both authors studied with Lloyd Reynolds. See Bibliography for his writings and biography.)

SAMPLES

a few days ago I was introduced to an American colleague, a surgeon from New York. He immediately impressed me as most likeable, yet we had quite a

BEFORE
(July 1)

My soul has grown deep like rivers.
I bathed in the Euphrates when dawns were young.
I built my hut near the Congo
And it lulled me to sleep

AFTER
(July 22)

Barbara Charles, left-handed, "hook" position (See p.10)

the invention of writing and of a convenient system of records on paper has had a greater influence in uplifting the human race than any other

BEFORE

The invention of writing and of a convenient system of records on paper has had a greater influence in uplifting the human race than any other intellectual achievement in the career of man.

AFTER

Brian Stephenson (ten-week course)

The invention of writing and of a convenient system of records on paper has a greater influence race th achieve

BEFORE

Note: when copying "influence" the writer misread the l for an e.

The invention of writing and of a convenient. System of records on paper has a greater infeuence in uplifting the human race than any other intellectual

AFTER

Tom Seitz (ten-week course)

58

The pen is one of Man's most useful instruments of expression in the dissemination of knowledge and learning and

BEFORE
(Ten-week course, two hours of instruction per week.)

The pen is one of man's most useful instruments of expression in the dissemenation of knowlege

AFTER

Angel Petersen

The pen is one of man's most useful instruments of expression. In the dissem of knowledge and learning and in the

BEFORE

The pen is one of man's most useful instruments of expression. In the dissemination of knowledge and

AFTER

Gerald Asp (ten-week course)

Deal seven cards to each player. Place remaining cards in the center of the table. player to the left of the dealer plays any c prop

BEFORE

enjoy the delight of these kids as they write YOUR style — congrats again on your outstanding contribution — the books are fantabulous!!!

AFTER

Fran Strom

The system of writing which we have inherited from the Romans has had an influence in shaping our civilization

BEFORE

The system of writing which we have inherited from the Romans has had an influence in shaping our civilization

AFTER Caroline Holt (ten-week course)

Just want to let you know that your Penmanship Class helped me out a lot — I'm no longer ashamed of my handwriting. Happy Holidays!

Cindy Shields (ten-week course)

I also enjoy the aesthetic aspect of interjecting some art into my every-day work. As I and others look through the huge quantity of un-readable medical

Paul Jacobs, MD

Too often, the mere application of a broad-edged nib to letters yields an image that many find awesome, and then label "beautiful". I prefer to divide calligraphy a bit from handwriting in the interest of attaining a method of communication that is not daunting.

Nan Jay Barchowsky

yes I'd like some surprise book & bamboo pen handouts

Carol Erickson

I have enjoyed the Italic Handwriting Series & the workshop that I took

Meilan Hom

I alternate between the one and two stroke-e, with no particular pattern.

Scot Heter

PART THREE

Edged Pen Italic

Italic Handwriting with the Edged Pen

Basic Italic

Cursive Italic

Chancery Cursive

Pangrams

Personal Correspondence

Greeting Card and Booklet

Samples

ITALIC HANDWRITING WITH THE EDGED PEN
writing tools/inks/papers/how to sit/pen hold & pen angle

WRITING WITH AN EDGED PEN will help make your handwriting look handsome, beautiful, official! You'll need to spend time developing the correct pen hold and using the letters — but you'll probably find it will be well worth the cost of pen, ink & paper. You can bring yourself and others pleasure through your writing.

WRITING TOOLS

Many edged tools are available — fiber and felt-tip pens, cartridge ink pens, fountain pens and dip nibs. (A nib is a pen tip.) You can also cut your own pens from ice cream sticks, tongue depressors, paint stir sticks, cattail stalks, green garden stakes, bamboo reeds, etc. A few are shown below:

The left-handed person may find left oblique nibs helpful, but the square cut nibs can be used.

  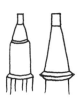 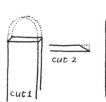

FOUNTAIN PENS   PENHOLDERS WITH DIP NIBS   FIBER-TIP PENS   TONGUE DEPRESSOR   CATTAIL STALK
(for large letters)

INKS

Be sure to use fountain pen ink in fountain pens. If you're using a dip nib, use ink that is <u>not</u> waterproof (unless you need your writing waterproofed). Waterproof inks generally contain shellac and tend to clog dip pens — and ruin fountain pens. You can learn to write with any kind of ink. Be sure to stir the bottle before using and replace the cap after each use. Black and many colors are available. Try mixing two colors of the same type and brand to create your own color.

PAPERS

For practice, white typing paper or a bond paper will usually provide a suitable writing surface. Avoid onionskin and easy-to-erase paper. The best way to select paper is to write on a sample piece to see if it takes ink well and does not feather. Colored papers can add interest to your writing — try colored butcher paper for large signs. Construction paper is usually too rough and porous. Most papers are machine made, but a few are made by hand. See pp. 36, 37 and 40 for more information about papermaking.

Both letters 1 & 2 were written with the same pen on different paper. 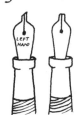 feathering

HOW TO SIT

Rest your forearms on the writing surface, feet flat on the floor and keep your back comfortably straight as you lean slightly forward.

It is easier to get the entire edge of your pen nib on the surface of your paper if you write on a slanted board.

If you are left-handed, try either paper position A, B, or somewhere in between. If you write from above the line, hold paper similar to C or D.

If you are right-handed, use paper position C for rapid everyday writing. For careful (formal) work, hold paper as in D.

PEN HOLD & ANGLE

Hold your pen with thumb and index finger resting it on the middle finger. Rest the shaft near the large knuckle.

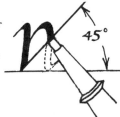 45°

Pen edge lies at 45° angle to the writing line. This allows pen edge to form the correct thicks and thins as you write lowercase letters.

BASIC ITALIC

GUIDE-LINES

The body height of italic lower-case letters is generally four or five pen widths regardless of the size of the pen. The pen is held horizontally to mark off the pen widths to measure the distance between guidelines.

Guidelines:

BASIC ITALIC   CURSIVE ITALIC

ascender line
waist line   45°
base line   body height   ascender → cap   ascender → cap
descender line   aghfP · aghfP
                          ←descender   ←descender

In this book the ascender and descender lines are not shown since ascenders and descenders have been shortened. The shortened letters allow you to write faster. If you are carefully writing out a poem, quotation, etc., you may wish to extend your ascenders and descenders to 4 or 5 pen widths each.

Caps are always written 1½ times body height of lower-case.

EXTRA FINE | Calligraphy –beautiful writing.

extended ascenders and descenders

BASIC STROKES

45°

Don't shift pen or arm – keep pen edge at a constant pen angle to the base line.

+ + + + ⋀⋀⋀ //// ⋋⋋⋋ XXXX mm uuu

Trace & copy

BASIC ITALIC

ii jj ll · kk or kk vv ww xx zz ·

See pages 14 to 17 for lower-case families.

hh mm nn rr · uu yy · bb pp

To write the size shown on lines 1-13, use a fine nib. Dip nibs are also available in this size.

aa dd gg qq · e or e oo cc ss · ff tt

See page 18 for capital families.

CDGOQ · MW · AHKNTUVXYZ
overlap at A & B

Flatten pen edge angle between 15°–30° for caps. (But stay at 45° for rapid writing.)

15°

EFLBPRRS JJ · 0123456789 · . , ? ! " "

Alphabet Sentence

A quick brown fox jumps over the lazy dog.
or k

* To flatten pen edge angle to 15°–30°, keep the __same__ pen hold, but:
   LEFT-HANDED · move elbow away from your body to flatten pen edge angle.
   RIGHT-HANDED · move right elbow closer to your body.

4mm

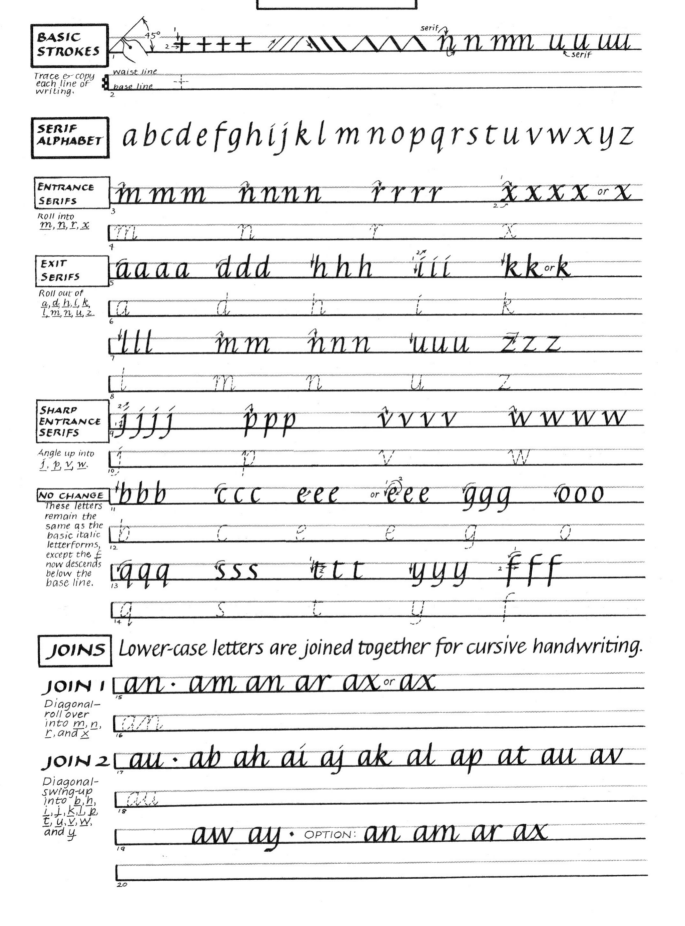

CURSIVE ITALIC

BASIC STROKES

Trace & copy each line of writing.

waist line
base line

SERIF ALPHABET

a b c d e f g h i j k l m n o p q r s t u v w x y z

ENTRANCE SERIFS

Roll into m, n, r, x

m m m   n n n n   r r r   x x x x or x

EXIT SERIFS

Roll out of a, d, h, i, k, l, m, n, u, z.

a a a a   d d d   h h h   i i i   k k or k

l l l   m m   n n   u u u   z z z

SHARP ENTRANCE SERIFS

Angle up into j, p, v, w.

j j j j   p p p   v v v v   w w w w

NO CHANGE
These letters remain the same as the basic italic letterforms, except the f now descends below the base line.

b b b   c c c   e e e or e e e   g g g   o o o

q q q   s s s   t t t   y y y   f f f

JOINS   Lower-case letters are joined together for cursive handwriting.

JOIN 1

Diagonal-roll over into m, n, r, and x.

an · am an ar ax or ax

JOIN 2

Diagonal-swing-up into b, h, i, j, k, l, p, t, u, v, w, and y

au · ab ah ai aj ak al ap at au av

aw ay · OPTION: an am ar ax

JOIN 3
Diagonal-start back into o and s

ao · ao as · OPTION: ae

JOIN 4
Diagonal into e

ae · ae ee ie ue te

JOIN 5
Horizontal out of f, o, t, v, w, and x

on · fn on tn vn wn xn

JOIN 6
Diagonal out of r

rn · ra re ri ro ru rz

JOIN 7
Horizontal to diagonal out of b, p, and s

sn · bn pn sn

JOIN 8
Diagonal into horizontal top of a, c, d, g, q, and s

aa · aa ac ad ag aq as

LIFTS
Lift before f and z.
Lift after g, j, q, & y.

af az · gn jn qu yn

EXERCISE

ana bnb cnc dnd ene fnf gng hnh ini

For more practice with joins, see pages 33 to 43. Use lines on page 91 or 93 as a liner sheet under your writing paper.

jnj knk lnl mnm nnn ono pnp qnq rnr

sns tnt unu vnv wnw xnx yny & znz

SENTENCE PRACTICE

Certainly the art of writing is the most

Thomas Carlyle 1795-1881 Scottish essayist & historian

miraculous of all things man has devised.

4mm

~: Examples for training the Hand :~
A ·aabcdiee'fcg hiklmnopqpg
orsʃtuxxyz̄ ɛt ʃt ʃʃʃ ʃʃ ʃti ww

No Glory comes at the Start, but at the end.
Thus is born honor, true &
perfect:
Why enter the field of battle, & then flee'?

Jlle Jdem & Vicetinus Scribebat Rome'.

Translation by John Howard Benson of LA OPERINA by Ludovico degli Arrighi, Rome, 1522. THE FIRST WRITING BOOK by John Howard Benson (Yale University Press, 1955.) Reproduced by permission.

Writing with an edged pen at a 45° angle creates a thin line for the diagonal join—a pleasing contrast.

an

For a thinner horizontal line, flatten the pen edge angle slightly for the crossbar of f and t and also for Join 5 (similar to pen edge angle for capitals, page 63).

CURSIVE CAPITALS

A B C D E F F G H I or II J or JJ K

L M N O P Q R R S T U or U V

15°

Flatten pen edge angle between 15° and 30° for carefully written caps. Stay at 45° for rapid writing.

W X Y or Y or Y or Y Z · Use these caps with lower-case only. Don't write entire words with these caps.

Lower-case joins:

abcdefghijklmnopqrstuvwxyz

CAPITAL PRACTICE

Amazon Brazos Columbia Danube

Principal rivers of the world written with a size fine nib.

Euphrates Fraser Ganges Huang Ho

OPTION: *You may prefer a 2-stroke e with the edged pen,*

ae ae *with flourish out of e.*

Indus Juruá Kolyma Loire or Loire *two-stroke e*

Mississippi Nile Orinoco Paraná

Quarai Rhine Snake Tigrus Ural

OPTION: *You may prefer to begin i, u, and y with a serif.*

i, u, y

Volga White Xingu Yukon Zambezi

4mm

SENTENCE PRACTICE

Written with a size extra fine nib.

3mm lines are on pages 95 and 96.

A true source of human happiness lies in taking a genuine interest in all the details of daily life and elevating them by art. WILLIAM MORRIS

3mm

CHANCERY CURSIVE · In the 15th and 16th centuries, the chancery cursive hand developed. The chancery was the office where official documents were kept, and chancery cursive was the official handwriting for these records.

A Flourish is a flowing curve.

Beginning serifs on i, u, y:

FLOURISHED ASCENDERS & DESCENDERS

bb dd hh kk ll ff gg jj pp ii uu yy

ASCENDERS: With dip pen, move slightly to the right before moving left.

CHANCERY LOWERCASE

abcdefghijklmnopqrstuvwxyz

Trace & write:
NOTE: Ascenders are taller and descenders are longer.

CHANCERY CAPITALS

AABBCCDDEEFFGG

For carefully written caps, flatten pen edge angle to 15°–30°. Stay at 45° for rapid writing.

GG HH II or II JJ or JJ KKLL

← Be sure this is a sharp angle on H, K, M, N, U, V, W.

MMNNOOPPQQ QQ RR

Keep horizontals straight except for slight curve at A & B.

SSTTUUVVWWXYYZ

There are many different choices of chancery caps.

SENTENCE PRACTICE

Arrighi's La Operina

the first italic instruc

tion manual, was pub

lished in Rome in 1522.

The first italic instruction book was written by Ludovico degli Arrighi (Vincentino).
It is printed from wood blocks, therefore, it is thought the letters appear more angular than the actual handwriting of that time.

Remember, your handwriting is a personal statement. For careful (formal) writing, you may choose to use fewer joins.

·: Exempli per firmar la Mano :—
A·cabcdeefeg hiklmnopqpg orsstuxyyz. Et St ff ſſ ßfu ʋw

No e' Gloria il principio, ma il seguir'. De' qu nasce' l'honor uero. &
perfit to:
Che' vale in campo intrare, et poi fuggire'?

Ille' Idem. L. Vicetinus Scribebat Romę.

From LA OPERINA by Ludovico degli Arrighi, Rome, 1522. THE FIRST WRITING BOOK by John Howard Benson (Yale University Press, 1955.) Reproduced by permission. [Translation on page 65.]

EDGED PEN ITALIC

PANGRAMS

Each sentence contains all 26 letters of the alphabet.

BASIC ITALIC

Quick wafting zephyrs vex bold Jim.

NOTE:
2-stroke k
on line 1;
1-stroke k
on line 3.

Picking just six quinces, new farmhand proves strong but lazy.

A large fawn jumped quickly over white zinc boxes.

CURSIVE ITALIC

Fred specialized in the job of making very quaint wax trays.

NOTE:
2-stroke e
in "very."

NOTE:
Lift after
w in "vowed."

Six crazy kings vowed to abolish my quite pitiful jousts.

Jack amazed a few girls and boys by dropping the antique onyx vase.

4mm

PANGRAMS,
continued

Many big jackdaws quickly zipped
over the fox pen.

M

Five or six big jet planes zoomed
quickly by the new tower.

F

CHANCERY CURSIVE

Waltz, nymph, for quick jigs vex Bud.

W

NOTE:
2-stroke e
in "vex'd."

Frowzy things plumb vex'd Jack Q.

I quickly explained that many big
jobs involve few hazards.

J

UNJOINED CHANCERY

A quick brown fox jumps over the lazy dog.

A

Quickly pack the box with five dozen
modern jugs.

Q

See p. 11 for further information on the Dubay/Getty calligraphy manual—ITALIC LETTERS: CALLIGRAPHY AND HANDWRITING.

4mm

PERSONAL CORRESPONDENCE

One of the anticipations of each weekday is checking the mail. How grand it is when we receive a handwritten message from a friend. You can bring joy into the lives of others with a cheery note or letter — and you can practice your handwriting at the same time. Surprise a friend with your words!

Use them for letters. Write on! • Dear Reader, Not all letters have to be written on standard sizes sheets of paper. Sometimes print shops will sell or give you endcuts.

WRITE LETTERS ON LONG STRIPS

Sometimes messages can be written at random.

Not all of your correspondence has to be designed the same.

Dan

Put a surprise in the envelope by designing your own format.

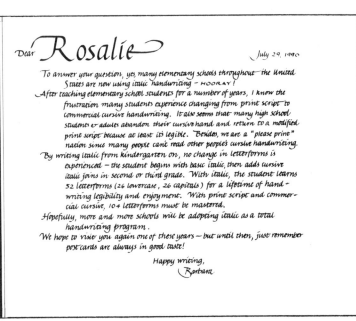

Dear Rosalie   July 29, 1990

To answer your question, yes, many elementary schools throughout the United States are now using italic handwriting — HOORAY!

After teaching elementary school students for a number of years, I know the frustration many students experience changing from print script to commercial cursive handwriting. It also seems that many high school students & adults abandon their cursive hand and return to a modified print script because at least it's legible. Besides, we are a "please print" nation since many people can't read other people's cursive handwriting.

By writing italic from kindergarten on, no change in letterforms is experienced — the student begins with basic italic, then adds cursive italic joins in second or third grade. With italic, the student learns 52 letterforms (26 lowercase, 26 capitals) for a lifetime of handwriting legibility and enjoyment. With print script and commercial cursive, 104 letterforms must be mastered.

Hopefully, more and more schools will be adopting italic as a total handwriting program.

We hope to visit you again one of these years — but until then, just remember post cards are always in good taste!

Happy writing,
Barbara

There's more to it than just wiggling your fingers and out come the letters

Dear Dan,
I understand you're learning italic handwriting. TERRIFIC! One of the best ways to exercise your new skill is by writing notes and letters to your friends. You might write a short quote on the left with a wider pen, then the text at the right as I have written here.
Love, Barbara
15 · IX · 90

HOWARD GLASSER

ENVELOPES

Design your own envelope by using a commercial envelope for a pattern. Cut your envelopes from plain paper, gift wrap paper, or large magazine covers. For the last two papers, use a self-sticking label for the address & attach the stamp with adhesive.

Margaret
420 JFK BLVD
PHILADELPHIA
PA · 17614

2763 N. Beach Drive
ROGER BAIN
Catalina · CA · 98761

MARTIN · MAR Beverly TIN · MARTIN · MARTIN
572 POLK AVENUE
MIAMI · FL · 12345

Chuck
Vernon
Chuck
Vernon
Chuck
Vernon
CHUCKVERNON
Chuck 25 Murray, Atlanta, GA 47561
Vernon
Chuck
Vernon
Chuck

HAPPY
BIRTHDAY
HAPPY
BIRTHDAY
Arlene Robs
723 S. Elm
Boise, ID 11136
BIRTHDAY

quoted with permission of Howard Glasser

Note: The state and zip code should be written on the same line.

GREETING CARD

(birthday, get well, friendship, anniversary) To make a greeting card for business size envelope, 10.5 cm x 24 cm (4⅛"x 8½"), you will need :
scissors · yarn or thread, 90 cm (35½") · needle · ruler · paperclips
1 sheet typing paper or similar cut to 19 cm x 22 cm (7½" x 8¾") for inside card
1 sheet colored paper (heavier than typing) cut to 20 cm x 23 cm (8"x 9") for cover of card

ⓐ Fold both sheets lengthwise & crease.
ⓑ Insert typing paper inside cover.
ⓒ Paperclip sheets together.
ⓓ On the inside, make a center dot A and one on either side at equal distances from the center, BC.
ⓔ Push needle through the 3 dots ABC to establish stitching holes.
ⓕ Stitch sheets together as follows :
　1) From outside cover, pass needle through center hole A, leaving 15 cm (6") for tying.
　2) From inside, pass needle through hole B to outside of card.
　3) From outside, skip over A, pass needle through third hole C to inside.
　4) From inside, pass needle through center hole A to outside.
　5) Tie knot over the long stitch. Cut ends to 4 or 5 cm (approx. 1½" or 2") or instead of cutting ends, tie in bow as shown.
Complete cover & inside message before or after stitching.

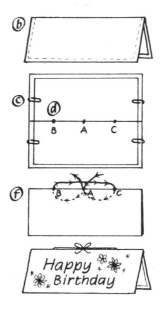

THE SURPRISE BOOKLET

Use as a small booklet, greeting card, or personal note.
Materials: any size sheet of light or medium weight paper and scissors.
A 21.5 cm x 28 cm (8½"x 11") sheet will give a finished size of 7cm x 10.8 cm (2¾" x 4¼").
A 21.5 cm x 35.5 cm (8½"x 14") sheet will give a finished size of 9 cm x 10.8 cm (3½" x 4¼").
A 28 cm x 43 cm (11"x 17") sheet will give a finished size of 10.8 cm x 14 cm (4¼" x 5½").
A completed booklet from the 11"x 17" sheet will fit an A-2 envelope (4⅜"x 5¾").

NOTE: In illustrations below, dotted line indicates fold that occurs within the given step. Solid lines within rectangle indicate folds previously established.

① Fold AB to CD to establish EF.

② Open back to original size.

③ Fold AC to BD to establish GH.

④ Fold GH to AC/BD to establish IJ.

⑤ Open to previous fold (GH/AB/CD).

⑥ With scissors, cut KL by cutting halfway between GH, stopping at fold IJ.

⑦ Open to original size ABCD.

⑧ Refold AB to CD as in ①.

⑨ Grasp E/AC with left hand and F/BD with right hand, then push hands together, establishing 3 pages on one side and 1 on the other.

⑩ Fold remaining leaf over the other three pages. Two leaves have folds at the top and two on the fore edge of the booklet.

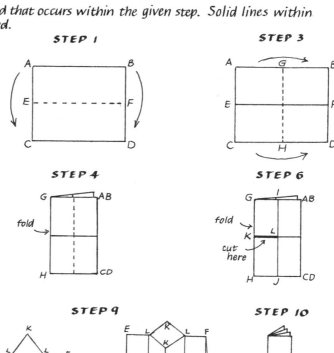

SAMPLES

Your postal service is as good as ours.

    I dislike my octagenarian handwriting.

My pen has its own waywardness.

    I trust you are well.

       Yours sincerely

        Alfred Fairbank

Alfred Fairbank

The Earth renews itself daily

Bill Gunderson

I hope this finds you well !
It is almost a year since we met
and christmas has found me
without my usual card but I

Tom Gourdie

Good talking to you — always a joy !

Maury Nemoy

Barbara, your card is magnificent! Did
Jaki tell you that Fairbank wrote that
he is including your Italic in his exhibition,
which will be shown in Rome, Milan,
Naples, & Bologna. You're now inter—
national !

       warmest regards to all,

       Lloyd

Lloyd Reynolds

Probably the three most important characteristics of
legible italic cursive are : 1. the two-stroke e, 2. the
elliptical arch & 3. the elimination of loops.

Jacqueline Svaren

What a deee lightful surprise
to get that gigantic box of material
on handwriting — a very smart move
because you hit me right at home — as
a Lloyd-bred calligrapher & mother
of wee-ones. Am already sending

Eliza Schulte

I have just received your parcel of
eight handwriting books by surface mail.
I must say I am impressed with them!

Christopher Jarman

I really liked
teaching Italic to adults ... &
they were so appreciative &
receptive!

Mary Kuhn Nash

please keep those cards & letters
coming as you're a good motivator

Don Butler

After 5 years of retirement, time,
in the form of diaries, calendars & regulated schedules,
has ceased to matter very much, so getting a Christmas
card in July gives just as much pleasure as in December.
Thank you for persevering!

Les Bennett, left-handed

73

I really enjoyed the workshop. This is about the fourth I've attended, and – I think – the best so far. I know some of that has to do with my own "seasoning" process.

Lorna Hutsell

I would also appreciate your observations on starting a program – what to stress, what to watch out for, what

Don Fluharty

has been helpful. i enjoyed talking with you. persevere.

Charlie Blank

Mary Worthington

this one has my greetings and best wishes to you

The boys are changing rapidly as they grow older, and our responsibilities toward them increase as their interests expand fourfold.

Kay Fujita

Do hope you are up here again – The clavichord is nestling beside the harpsichord. Certainly has a delicate sound ——

Noreen Monroe Guzie

what the future holds? Hopefully, italic handwriting in our schools!

Laurie Broadhurst

I could feel Lois standing there with us, smiling and approving. Thank you, thank you. Love, Edie

Edie Roberts

Write on! Barbara Getty

Write now! Inga Dubay

PART FOUR

Development of Our Alphabet

Capitals and Lower-case
Impact of the Major Historical Scripts

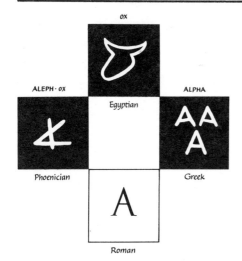

Egyptian hieroglyph ☒ representing "ox"
Phoenician letter ∢ name ALEPH "ox"
Early Greek name ALPHA A RIGHT TO LEFT A LEFT TO RIGHT
→∢A Boustrophēdon, Greek "ox turning" Lines change
→AB< direction alternately. After c.500 BC left to right only.
Classical Greek A
Early Roman A; Imperial Roman A

DEVELOPMENT OF LOWER-CASE A

ʌ ʌ ɑ ɑ ɑ a a
Rustic Uncial Half-Uncial Carolingian Gothic Humanist Italic

Aa Aa
Basic Italic   Cursive Italic

Egyptian hieroglyphs ☐ ☐ ☐ "house"
Phoenician letter 9 name BETH "house"
Early Greek name BETA ꓭ RIGHT TO LEFT B LEFT TO RIGHT
Classical Greek B
Early Roman B; Imperial Roman B

DEVELOPMENT OF LOWER-CASE B

ß ʙ b b b b h
Rustic Uncial Half-Uncial Carolingian Gothic Humanist Italic

Bb Bb
Basic Italic   Cursive Italic

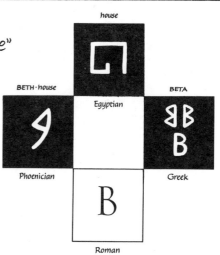

Phoenician letter ↑
  name GIMEL "camel"
Early Greek > RIGHT TO LEFT < LEFT TO RIGHT
Classical Greek Γ
Early Roman C
Imperial Roman C

The Romans added a bar to
C to form G in order to differentiate sounds. G was
added to the alphabet in
the 3rd century B.C.

Early Roman G
Imperial Roman G

DEVELOPMENT OF LOWER-CASE C

C c c c c c c
Rustic Uncial Half-Uncial Carolingian Gothic Humanist Italic

C c C c
Basic Italic   Cursive Italic

DEVELOPMENT OF LOWER-CASE G

G ç ȝ g g g g
Rustic Uncial Half-Uncial Carolingian Gothic Humanist Italic

Gg Gg
Basic Italic   Cursive Italic

The development of the alphabet is based on ANCIENT WRITING AND ITS INFLUENCES by Berthold Louis Ullman

Egyptian hieroglyph ⅢⅢ representing "door"
Phoenician letter △ name DALETH "door"
Early Greek name DELTA ◁ *RIGHT TO LEFT* ▷ *LEFT TO RIGHT*
Classical Greek △
Early Roman D; Imperial Roman D

DEVELOPMENT OF LOWER-CASE D

Ɔ ꝺ d d d d

Rustic Uncial Half-Uncial Carolingian Gothic Humanist Italic

Dd Dd

Basic Italic Cursive Italic

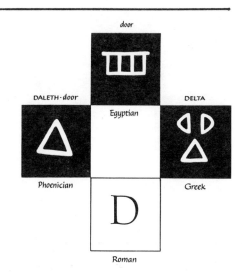

door

Egyptian

DALETH · door — Phoenician

DELTA — Greek

D — Roman

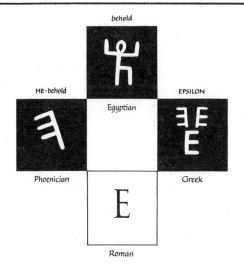

behold

Egyptian

HE · behold — Phoenician

EPSILON — Greek

E — Roman

Egyptian hieroglyphs 𓀠 𓀟 𓀞 "behold"
Phoenician letter ⅃ name HE "behold"
Early Greek name EPSILON
Ⅎ *RIGHT TO LEFT* Ⅎ *LEFT TO RIGHT*
Early Roman E; Imperial Roman E

DEVELOPMENT OF LOWER-CASE E

ɛ e e e e e

Rustic Uncial Half-Uncial Carolingian Gothic Humanist Italic

Ee Ee

Basic Italic Cursive Italic

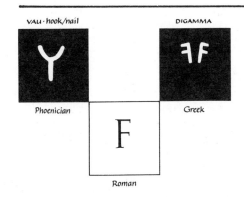

VAU · hook/nail — Phoenician

DIGAMMA — Greek

F — Roman

Phoenician letter Y name VAU "hook, nail"
Early Greek name DIGAMMA Ⅎ *RIGHT TO LEFT* F *LEFT TO RIGHT*
Early Roman F; Imperial Roman F

DEVELOPMENT OF LOWER-CASE F

ſ ſ ꜰ f f f

Rustic Uncial Half-Uncial Carolingian Gothic Humanist Italic

Ff Ff

Basic Italic Cursive Italic

TIMELINE

						CLASSICAL GREEK	UNCIAL HALF-UNCIAL		ITALIC HUMANIST
			EARLY GREEK			IMPERIAL ROMAN		GOTHIC	
EGYPTIAN		PHOENICIAN				EARLY ROMAN RUSTIC		CAROLINGIAN	

3000 B.C. 2500 B.C. 2000 B.C. 1500 B.C. 1000 B.C. 500 B.C. 0 A.D. 500 A.D. 1000 A.D. 1500 A.D. 2000

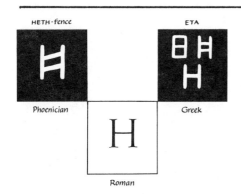

Phoenician letter Ⱶ name CHETH "fence"
Early Greek name ETA ⊟ or Ⱶ
Classical Greek H
Early Roman Ⱶ; Imperial Roman H

DEVELOPMENT OF LOWER-CASE H

Rustic Uncial Half-Uncial Carolingian Gothic Humanist Italic

Hh Hh

Basic Italic   Cursive Italic

Egyptian hieroglyph ⟿ "hand"
Phoenician letter Ⰶ name YOD
    name YOD "hand"   "hand"
Early Greek name IOTA Ⰶ RIGHT TO LEFT
    Ⰶ LEFT TO RIGHT; Classical Greek I
Early Roman I
Imperial Roman I

DEVELOPMENT OF LOWER-CASE I & J

Rustic Uncial Half-Uncial Carolingian Gothic Humanist Italic

Ii   I OR Ji   Jj   J OR Jj

Basic Italic   Cursive Italic   Basic Italic   Cursive Italic

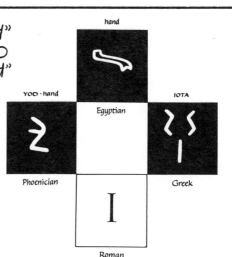

J is originally a variant of the letter I (long j). It was formally added to the alphabet in the 16th century.

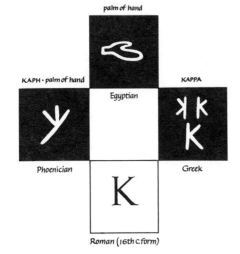

Egyptian hieroglyph ⬭ "palm"
Phoenician letter Ɣ KAPH "palm"
Early Greek name KAPPA
    Ⱪ RIGHT TO LEFT   K LEFT TO RIGHT; Classical Greek K
Early Roman K; Imperial Roman K
    K was rarely used.

DEVELOPMENT OF LOWER-CASE K

Rustic Uncial Half-Uncial Carolingian Gothic Humanist Italic

Kk OR k   Kk

Basic Italic   Cursive Italic

Egyptian hieroglyph "ox goad, cudgel"
Phoenician letter name LAMED
"ox goad, cudgel"
Early Greek name LAMBDA or RIGHT TO LEFT
or LEFT TO RIGHT; Classical Greek Λ
Early Roman L; Imperial Roman L

DEVELOPMENT OF LOWER-CASE L

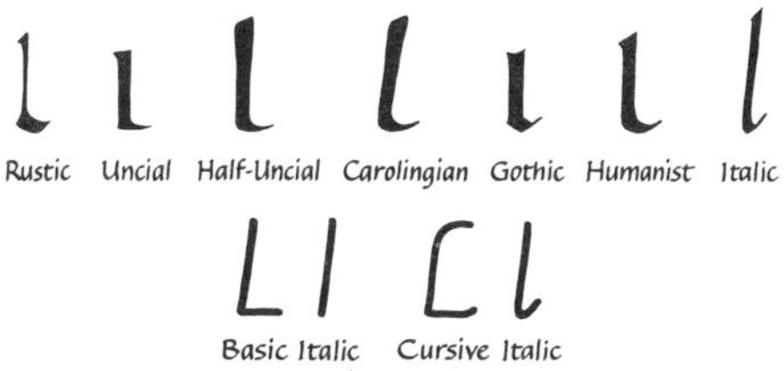
Rustic
Uncial
Half-Uncial
Carolingian
Gothic
Humanist
Italic
Basic Italic
Cursive Italic

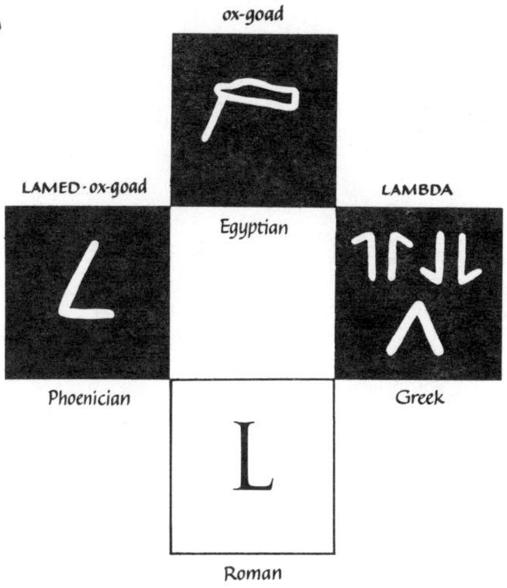
ox-goad
LAMED · ox-goad
Egyptian
LAMBDA
Phoenician
Greek
L
Roman

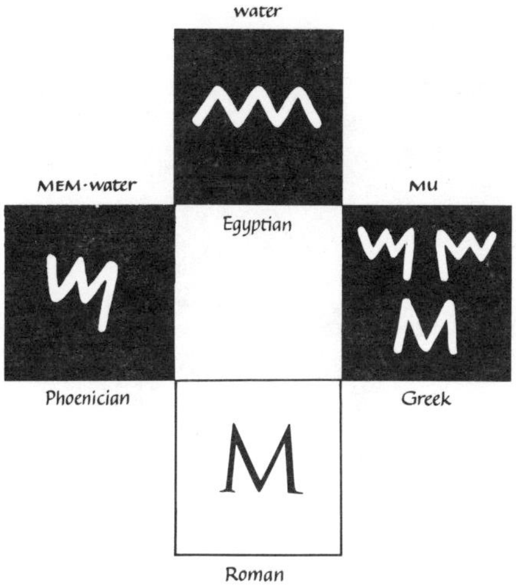
water
MEM · water
Egyptian
MU
M
Phoenician
Greek
M
Roman

Egyptian hieroglyphs "water"
Phoenician letter name MEM "water"
Early Greek name MU RIGHT TO LEFT LEFT TO RIGHT
Classical Greek M
Early Roman; Imperial Roman M

DEVELOPMENT OF LOWER-CASE M

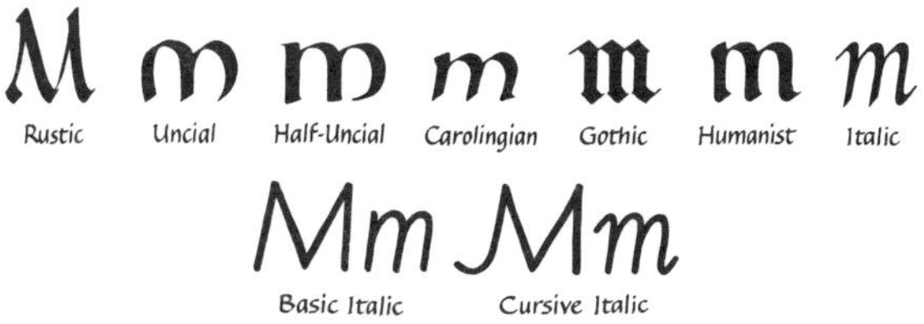
Rustic
Uncial
Half-Uncial
Carolingian
Gothic
Humanist
Italic
Mm Mm
Basic Italic
Cursive Italic

Egyptian hieroglyph "fish"
Phoenician letter NUN "fish"
Early Greek name NU RIGHT TO LEFT
LEFT TO RIGHT; Classical Greek N
Early Roman N; Imperial N

DEVELOPMENT OF LOWER-CASE N

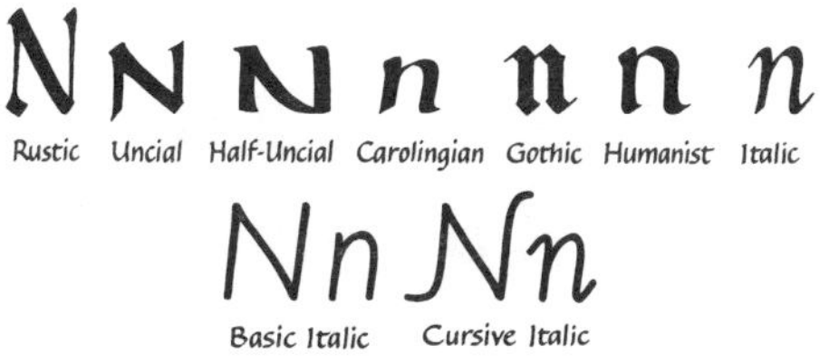
Rustic
Uncial
Half-Uncial
Carolingian
Gothic
Humanist
Italic
Nn Nn
Basic Italic
Cursive Italic

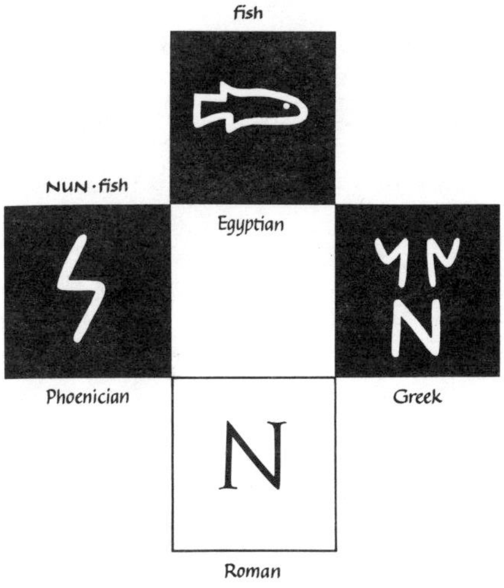
fish
NUN · fish
Egyptian
N
Phoenician
Greek
N
Roman

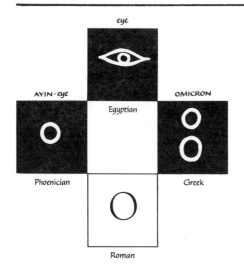

eye

Egyptian

AYIN - eye | OMICRON

Phoenician | Greek

Roman

Egyptian hieroglyph ⬯ "eye"
Phoenician letter o name AYIN "eye" (written smaller than others)
Early Greek name OMICRON, O
Classical Greek O
Early Roman O; Imperial Roman O

O has changed the least of all the letters since c. 2000 B.C.

DEVELOPMENT OF LOWER-CASE O

O o o o o o o o

Rustic Uncial Half-Uncial Carolingian Gothic Humanist Italic

O o O o

Basic Italic   Cursive Italic

Egyptian hieroglyph ⬯ "mouth"
Phoenician letter ⌐ name PE "mouth"
Early Greek letter PI ⌐ RIGHT TO LEFT   ⌐ LEFT TO RIGHT or ⌐, ⌐
Classical Greek ⊓
Early Roman ⌐; Imperial Roman P

DEVELOPMENT OF LOWER-CASE P

f r p p p p p

Rustic Uncial Half-Uncial Carolingian Gothic Humanist Italic

P p P p

Basic Italic   Cursive Italic

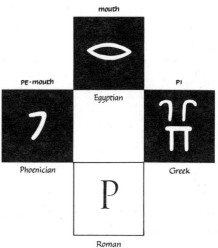

mouth

Egyptian

PE - mouth | PI

Phoenician | Greek

Roman

Phoenician letter ⌐ name QOPH "knot"
Early Greek name KOPPA *(Dropped from Classical Greek.)*
Early Roman Q ; Imperial Roman Q

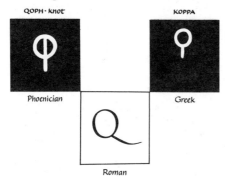

QOPH - knot | KOPPA

Phoenician | Greek

Roman

DEVELOPMENT OF LOWER-CASE Q

Q q q q q q q

Rustic Uncial Half-Uncial Carolingian Gothic Humanist Italic

Q q Q q

Basic Italic   Cursive Italic

Egyptian hieroglyph ⟨⟩ "head"
Phoenician letter ⟨⟩ name RESH "head"
Early Greek letter RHO ⟨⟩ *RIGHT TO LEFT* P *LEFT TO RIGHT*
Classical Greek P or R
Early Roman P R; Imperial Roman R

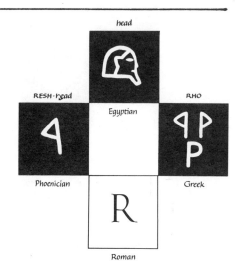

DEVELOPMENT OF LOWER-CASE R

Ŕ Ŕ ſ ſ ſ ſ r

Rustic   Uncial   Half-Uncial   Carolingian   Gothic   Humanist   Italic

Rr   Rr

Basic Italic   Cursive Italic

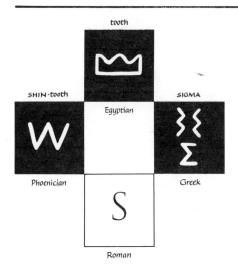

Egyptian hieroglyphs ⟨⟩ ⟨⟩ "tooth"
Phoenician letter W name SHIN "tooth"
Early Greek name SIGMA ⟨⟩ *RIGHT TO LEFT* ⟨⟩ *LEFT TO RIGHT*
Classical Greek Σ
Early Roman S; Imperial Roman S

DEVELOPMENT OF LOWER-CASE S

S s ſ ſ ſ ſ ſ

Rustic   Uncial   Half-Uncial   Carolingian   Gothic   Humanist   Italic

Ss   Ss

Basic Italic   Cursive Italic

Egyptian hieroglyphs ⟨⟩ X "mark"
Phoenician letter +, X name TAU "mark"
Early Greek name TAU T or T
Classical Greek T
Early Roman T; Imperial Roman T

DEVELOPMENT OF LOWER-CASE T

T ſ c t t t t

Rustic   Uncial   Half-Uncial   Carolingian   Gothic   Humanist   Italic

Tt   Tt

Basic Italic   Cursive Italic

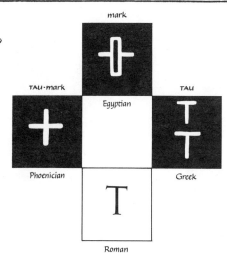

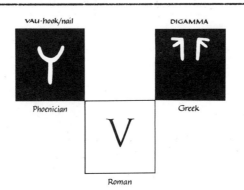

VAU·hook/nail

Phoenician

DIGAMMA

Greek

Roman

(16th c.form)

U *was the Medieval form of* V. *Both* U *and* V *were used interchangeably. In the 16th century* U *and* V *acquired their distinct pronounciations and* U *was formally added to the alphabet.*

Phoenician letter Y
   name VAU "hook, nail"
Early Greek ⅂ RIGHT TO LEFT ⌐ LEFT TO RIGHT
   name DIGAMMA
Early Roman V; Imperial V

W *was invented by the Germanic people, c. 11th century, to distinguish a sound close to, but different from* U. *Two* v's (u's) *were linked together to form a new letter.*

(16th c. form)

DEVELOPMENT OF LOWER-CASE U, V, & W

V   U   u   ww   uvw   uvw
Rustic Uncial Half-Uncial Carolingian   Gothic   Humanist   Italic

Uu   Uu   Vv   Vv   Ww   Ww
Basic Italic Cursive Italic Basic Italic Cursive Italic Basic Italic Cursive Italic

---

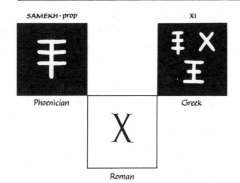

SAMEKH·prop

Phoenician

XI

Greek

Roman

Phoenician letter ‡ name SAMEKH "prop"
Early Greek ‡ or ⊞; Classical Greek:
   Western X name XI; Eastern ‡ name XI
Early Roman X; Imperial Roman X

DEVELOPMENT OF LOWER-CASE X

X   X   x   x   r   x   x
Rustic Uncial Half-Uncial Carolingian Gothic Humanist Italic

X   x   X   x
Basic Italic   Cursive Italic

Phoenician letter Y name VAU "hook, nail"
Early Greek Y (ㄱㄱ) DIGAMMA
Classical Greek Y UPSILON
Imperial Roman Υ *Added in the 1st century B.C. to transliterate Greek words.*

DEVELOPMENT OF LOWER-CASE Y

Y   Y   r   r   y   y   yy
Rustic Uncial Half-Uncial Carolingian Gothic Humanist   Italic

Yy   Yy
Basic Italic   Cursive Italic

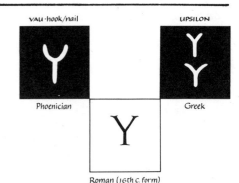

VAU·hook/nail

Phoenician

UPSILON

Greek

Roman (16th c. form)

Egyptian hieroglyph ⌐ "sickle, weapon"
Phoenician letter I name ZAYIN
    "sickle, weapon"
Early Greek I name ZETA
Classical Greek Z
Imperial Roman Z

Z was added in the
1st century B.C. to
transliterate
Greek words.

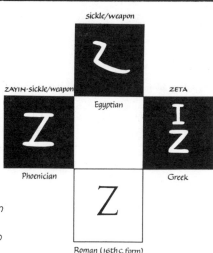

DEVELOPMENT OF LOWER-CASE Z

𝖑 z Z z ʒ Z Z
Rustic Uncial Half-Uncial Carolingian Gothic Humanist Italic

Zz Zz
Basic Italic Cursive Italic

ZETA was the sixth
letter of the Greek
alphabet. It was not
used in the Early Roman
alphabet and its place
was taken by G. When
it was added, it went to
the end of the alphabet.

IMPACT OF THE MAJOR HISTORICAL SCRIPTS

EGYPTIAN: *Invention of the acrophonic principle*   A picture of an object is used as a permanent representation for the initial letter of the word for the object.
2000 hieroglyphs of which 300 were common
Third millennium B.C. to A.D. 1st century

PHOENICIAN: *Creation of an alphabet using the acrophonic principle*
22 letters
Second millennium   ◻, ⅁ came to represent the letter B because that is the first letter of the Semitic word for house – BETH.

GREEK: *Addition of vowels* Many of the Greek names resemble the Phoenician names.
24 letters   (aleph — alpha; beth — beta)
Early: c. 1200 B.C. to 400 B.C.; Classical: c. 400 B.C. to A.D. 100

ROMAN: *Dissemination of the alphabet throughout the Roman Empire*
Early Roman: 21 letters; Imperial Roman: 23 letters
Early: 600 B.C. to 30 B.C.; Imperial: 30 B.C. to A.D. 500

RUSTIC: *Flowing version of Roman capitals*   Roman; 30 B.C. to A.D 5th century

UNCIAL: *Emerging ascenders and descenders*   Roman; 3rd to 9th centuries

HALF-UNCIAL: *Lengthening ascenders and descenders* Roman; 3rd to 9th centuries

CAROLINGIAN: *Use of large size letters as capitals and small size letters as lower-case* French, later international; 8th to 11th centuries

GOTHIC: *Use of the same pen for capitals and lower-case* European; 13th to 15th c.

HUMANIST: *Combination of legible letters and a simplified writing procedure* Italian; 15th to 16th centuries

ITALIC: *Cursive version of Humanist* Italian, English; 15th to 16th century

GLOSSARY

ASCENDER · The part of a letter that extends above the body height.

BASE LINE · The line on which letters "sit"; bottom line of body height. (Sometimes called writing line.)

BASIC ITALIC · A form of unjoined writing using italic letters without entrance or exit serifs.

BODY HEIGHT · The distance between base line & waist line. (Sometimes called "x height".)

BRANCHING LINE · An imaginary line in the center of the body height.

CALLIGRAPHY · Beautiful or elegant writing; also the art of producing such writing. The letters are generally unjoined and often written with the edged tool. Italic calligraphy is one type of formal hand lettering or writing.

CAPITAL LETTER · A letter in the series A, B, C, rather than a, b, c. (Sometimes called upper case, large letters, or caps.) Synonym: majuscule.

CHANCERY ITALIC · During the 15th and 16th centuries, the official handwriting of the chancery, the office where papal documents were kept.

COUNTER · The open area within a letter.

CROSSBAR · A horizontal line, second stroke of f and t.

CURSIVE ITALIC · A form of joined writing using italic letters with entrance and exit serifs. [Medieval Latin SCRIPTA CURSIVA—"flowing script"—from Latin CURSUS, past participle of CURRERE—"to run."] Four characteristics of a cursive hand are compressed (elliptical) forms, slight slope, fluent (branching for one-stroke letters) and joined letters.

DESCENDER · The part of a letter that extends below the base line and the body height.

DIAGONAL · A line from lower left to upper right (as used in joins & letter shapes) or a line from upper left to lower right (as used in letter shapes).

DOWNSTROKE · A line from top to bottom following letter slope angle.

ELLIPTICAL SHAPE · A line following a compressed circular shape or elongated circle (as in o).

HORIZONTAL · A line extending from left to right parallel to base line & waist line.

INTERSPACE · An area between letters within words.

ITALIC · A script originating in Italy in the late 15th and early 16th centuries. It is a slightly sloped, compressed, and fluent version of the 15th century humanist script. Italic was first called humanist cursive.

ITALIC HANDWRITING · A system of writing for everyday use incorporating both an unjoined form of writing (basic italic) and a cursive form of writing (cursive italic).

LETTER · SHAPE · The correct form of a capital or lower-case letter.
SIZE · The height or length of a letter.
SLOPE · The slant of a letter.
SPACING · The distance between letters in words.
SPEED · The rate of writing.
STROKES · The lines without lifts used to write a letter.

LOWER-CASE LETTER · A letter in the series a, b, c, rather than A, B, C. (Sometimes called small letters.) [From the printer's practice of keeping the small letters in the lower of a pair of type cases or drawers.] Synonym: minuscule.

PEN EDGE ANGLE · The angle of the edge of the pen nib in relation to the base line.

SERIF · An entrance or exit stroke of a letter.

UPPER CASE · See CAPITAL LETTER. [From the printer's practice of keeping the large letters in the upper of a pair of type cases or drawers.]

VERTICAL · A line from top to bottom following the slope line.

WAIST LINE · The top line of the body height.

BIBLIOGRAPHY

Anderson, Donald M. THE ART OF WRITTEN FORMS. New York: Holt, Rinehart and Winston, Inc. 1969.

Benson, John Howard. THE FIRST WRITING BOOK, AN ENGLISH TRANSLATION & FACSIMILE TEXT OF ARRIGHI'S Operina, THE FIRST MANUAL OF THE CHANCERY HAND. New Haven: Yale University Press, 1955.

Casson, Lionel & the editors of Time-Life Books. ANCIENT EGYPT, Great Ages of Man Series. New York: Time, Inc., 1965.

Catich, Edward M. THE ORIGIN OF THE SERIF. Davenport, Iowa: The Catfish Press, 1968.

Degering, Hermann. LETTERING. Berlin: Wasmuth, 1929.

Dubay, Inga, and Barbara Getty. ITALIC LETTERS: CALLIGRAPHY & HANDWRITING. New York: Prentice Hall Press. 1986. (originally published by Van Nostrand Reinhold Co., 1984.)

Edwards, Betty. DRAWING ON THE RIGHT SIDE OF THE BRAIN. Los Angeles: J.P. Tarcher, Inc., 1979.

—————. DRAWING ON THE ARTIST WITHIN. New York: Simon and Schuster, 1986.

Fairbank, Alfred, and R.W. Hunt. HUMANISTIC SCRIPT OF THE FIFTEENTH AND SIXTEENTH CENTURIES. Oxford: University Press, 1960.

Fairbank, Alfred. THE STORY OF HANDWRITING. New York: Watson-Guptill, 1970.

Fiore, Quentin. "Paper." INDUSTRIAL DESIGN: November, 1958.

Getty, Barbara, and Inga Dubay. ITALIC HANDWRITING SERIES, BOOKS A-G & INSTRUCTION MANUAL, second edition. Portland: Portland State University, Continuing Education Press, 1986.

Goudy, Frederic W. THE ALPHABET AND ELEMENTS OF LETTERING. New York: Dover, 1963.

Gourdie, Tom. ITALIC HANDWRITING. New York: Pentalic Corporation, 1976.

Gunderson, William and Charles Lehman. THE CALLIGRAPHY OF LLOYD J. REYNOLDS. Portland: The Alcuin Press, 1988.

Gürtler, Andre. THE DEVELOPMENT OF THE ROMAN ALPHABET. Switzerland: Bildungsverband Schweizerischer Buchdrucker. N.D.

Hayes, James. THE ROMAN LETTER. Chicago: The Lakeside Press. N.D.

Jackson, Donald. THE STORY OF WRITING. New York: Taplinger Publishing Company, 1981.

Jarman, Christopher J. THE DEVELOPMENT OF HANDWRITING SKILLS. Great Britain: Basil Blackwell, 1979.

Kim, Scott. INVERSIONS. Peterborough, N.H.: BYTE BOOKS, a division of McGraw Hill, 1981.

Lawrence, Sandra. "The Roman Inscriptional Letter." B.A. Thesis, Reed College, Portland, Oregon, 1955.

Lehman, Charles. HANDWRITING MODELS FOR SCHOOLS. Portland: The Alcuin Press, 1976.

McClelland, David. "The Curse of Commercial Cursive and Other Calligraphic Curiosities." HARPER'S MAGAZINE. June, 1975.

Moorhouse, A.C. THE TRIUMPH OF THE ALPHABET, A HISTORY OF WRITING. New York: Henry Schuman, 1953.

"Numerals," ENCYCLOPAEDIA BRITANNICA. Chicago: Encyclopaedia Britannica, Inc. 15th edition, 1980, XIII, 612-13.

Petersen, Karen, and J.J. Wilson. WOMEN ARTISTS: RECOGNITION & REAPPRAISAL FROM THE EARLY MIDDLE AGES TO THE TWENTIETH CENTURY. New York: New York University Press; Harper & Row, 1976.

Reynolds, Lloyd. "Handwriting and Calligraphy." OREGON RAINBOW. No. 4, 1976, pp. 32-39.

—————. Personal notes of Barbara Getty from lectures. Portland, Oregon, 1969-1977.

Shahn, Ben. LOVE AND JOY ABOUT LETTERS. New York: Grossman Publishers, 1963.

Skelly, Flora Johnson. "Grace Under Pressure." AMERICAN MEDICAL NEWS. February 23, 1990, p. 22.

Svaren, Jacqueline. WRITTEN LETTERS. New York: Taplinger Publishing Company, 1975.

Ullman, B.L. ANCIENT WRITING AND ITS INFLUENCE. New York: Cooper Square Publishers, Inc., 1963.

Von Eckardt, Wolf. PLEASE WRITE. New York: Atheneum, 1988.

—————. "Reforming with Zigs and Zags." TIME. March 21, 1983, p. 86.

Wallbank, T. Walter, and Alastair M. Taylor. CIVILIZATION, PAST AND PRESENT. Chicago: Scott, Foresman and Co., 1949.

We thank Ruth Ely and Olive Hilton for editing WRITE NOW.
We also thank Mark Van Stone for consultation on the development of the alphabet.
We would like to acknowledge the following authors for their contribution to today's interest in italic handwriting:

Kerstin Anckers
Gunnlaugur SE Briem
Fred Eager
Alfred Fairbank
Tom Gourdie
Charles Lehman
Lloyd Reynolds
Jacqueline Svaren
Wolf Von Eckardt
Irene Wellington

5° slope

Use the 5° slope lines on page 87 as a guide under notebook paper or under the writing lines on pages 89-96. Fasten sheets together with paper clips or tape.

Use the 5mm, 4mm, and 3mm writing lines on pages 89-96 as liner sheets under plain paper. You may prefer to write directly on the lines.

Permission is given to photocopy the slope lines on page 87 and the writing lines on pages 89-96 for personal use.

5mm

5mm

4mm

4mm

92

4mm

93

4mm